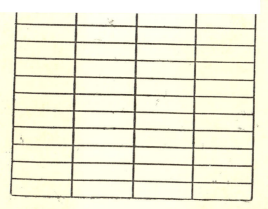

OH! FOR THE LIFE OF A COUNTRY GIRL

An Autobiography
1900–1984

by

Edna Holland Mitchell

BROADBLADE PRESS
11314 Miller Road
Swartz Creek, Michigan 48473

Typeset and printed in the United States of America
Sans Serif, Inc., and McNaughton & Gunn

Cover: October 3, 1918, Liberty Loan Day. The country school teacher at the wheel of her 1915 Patterson, in a jaunty mood, ready to take off for the Kline School to sell bonds.

Dedicated to my Family and Friends.
They have been an inspiration to me
throughout my life.

ABOUT THE BOOK

This is an unconventional autobiography. Edna Holland Mitchell's years of observation have totaled over eight decades. This happened to be a period in our history when tremendous change took place in every field of endeavor.

She has accurately recorded the effect that this progress has had on all humanity and on the families of country people specifically.

There is more information between the lines than in the paragraphs of type.

As a case in point, her life conforms to the liberation of womanhood. At the time she was born women were second class citizens. Few owned property or were allowed to have their names on deeds as joint owners. They could not vote, have a voice in government or hold public office. Higher education for girls was frowned upon as a waste of money.

With her positive attitude and the manner in which she faced situations Edna Mitchell was instrumental in showing the way in respect to women's rights without antagonizing anyone.

She came through the gate of her father's field walking barefoot in the dust behind a three-horse hitch of draft horses to become the first teenager in her community to drive an automobile in 1915 and the first young woman to own her own car in 1922. It was a Model T and cost $485. She was the first woman in the area to hold a major township office, a World War I Liberty Bond Salesperson, etc. The list is endless.

She has never been an activist or made the headlines as a result of a brash statement or action; however, in her own quiet manner, in cooperation with hundreds of other women of like nature, this goal of quality for women is within grasp.

Stanley Cozadd Perkins

CONTENTS

ACKNOWLEDGEMENTS

Ellen Brady
Silas, Olive and Sue Coquigne
Lillian Eddy
Myrtle Elie
Fred L. Fuller
Earl and Opal Hegel
Mary Lochman
Thomas Mitchell

Amanda Monroe
Joseph Myers Jr.
George and Hila O'Brien
Judith Parsons
Catherine Raubinger
Nelson Gerald Scott
Frank Sejak
Norma Rubey Steel

Edited by Mary Shaw

ILLUSTRATIONS

SCENE ALONG FLINT RIVER, FLINT, MICH.

Saginaw Street Bridge — a scene of contrasts: the hustle and bustle of modern industry and transportation side by side with the unhurried pace of a quiet boat ride.

FOREWORD

I would mention something that had happened in my younger days and my daughter Erma would say, "I didn't know that."

Thinking some of these happenings might be of interest to my family, I began jotting down a few things. As the notes piled up I accumulated many interesting memories, facts, records of historical events, and a few philosophical ideas for making life more interesting and less troublesome. They became the manuscript for this book. I trust that it will provide for you a peek into yesteryear.

When the Rev. David Rahn came to the South Mundy Methodist Church in June 1981, I was writing this book.

During a conversation with me he said, "You are a philosopher."

I thought that a philosopher must be an important person so I decided to consult Webster's to make sure he had me tagged right. Webster said, "One who lives after the principles of philosophy such as — practical wisdom, calmness, of even temper and judgement.

The Reverend could have been a bit benevolent. You be the judge. I live by my faith, optimism and enthusiasm.

This autobiography has been written by decades. There is an entwining of personal and public happenings with world affairs that took place at about the same time. This has a tendency to make the writing appear irregular but that is only the way it was — happy reading.

Edna Holland Mitchell

EDNA IRENE HOLLAND

At two years.

MY GRANDPARENTS

The Hollands

My paternal grandparents, John and Annie Holland, who were born in 1845 and 1854 respectively, came from North Devon, England. John's mother had worked very hard and saw no future for her children in England as it was nearly impossible for a person to become a home owner or landowner there. To keep the family's head above water financially, she would make things to sell, then row across the river where there were people to buy them.

While visiting England in 1970, I discovered that the land my ancestors had lived and worked on is now the location of a huge power plant.

John was one of about twelve children. As they grew to adulthood, John's mother insisted that they go to one of the newer countries. We never knew about any of them other than John. John married Annie Knill who lived not far away from the Hollands, and there was always contact with her family. They came to Flint Township, Michigan, on their wedding trip. There were friends of their family here who received them. They never

1

THE AUTHOR'S GRANDPARENTS in 1909

John Holland holding a pair of his good Angus family cows with his wife Anna Knill and their stock dog. This home is still in use with additions at 5347 W. Grand Blanc Road, Swartz Creek.

returned to England, even for a visit. It probably took all of their money just to get here.

John was a farmer. He worked as a hired hand, worked farms on shares, and then bought a 60 acre farm in Mundy Township on Grand Blanc Road. It is between Sharp and Linden Roads and now occupied by Robert and Barbara Whitaker. The farm still exists with some changes. They had an outside cellar that was built about one-half above ground and one-half below ground. It had thick stone walls with a half-pitch, shingled roof. About four steps down there was a dirt floor with a few boards laid down to walk on. It kept everything very cool. I don't think it froze down there in the winter. There was no cellar under the house, so it was the only place to keep food from spoiling.

John was a very good butcher, for himself as well as for other people. They had plenty of their own meat; such as lamb, pork, goose, duck, turkey, and chicken. At that time, people produced most of their own food and many other things they used. There were fruit trees, gardens and berries. They raised delicious gooseberries, which was something most people didn't have.

Annie was a wonderful cook. At that time, she was considered extravagant because she used the best of ingredients. I remember those delicious holiday dinners at Grandmother's table.

She was fond of very nice and pretty things. She always had pretty silk dresses. I think that she made them herself. She always had some money tucked away in various hiding places. She knew right where it was and the denomination.

There were five children: John Jr., Lillie, Frederick, Flora, and May who were my aunts and uncles.

John Jr.: When John, Jr., was about fourteen, he became blind. I think that he had some sort of sickness and was given either too strong or the wrong medicine, which caused the blindness. He went to the Lansing School for the Blind and learned Braille. I remember he would read to me when I was little. He made cord hammocks and bead trinkets. He lived at home and died in 1914 at the age of 37.

Lillie: Lillie married William Wiggins and had six children: Frank, Clarence, John, Earl, Herbert and Alice.

Frederick: Frederick was born June 30, 1877. He was my father and he married Eva McTaggart. I, Edna, am the only child.

Flora: Flora married Wesley Kimball and had one daughter, Nellie.

Mae: Mae married Jacob Berdan and had two children, Claude and Florence.

John and Annie sold the farm in their later years, had an auction sale and moved to Swartz Creek in 1919. John was a hard worker and kept busy cutting wood along the creek bank. He died three years later in 1921 following an injury to his leg that he had received while wood-cutting.

Annie had bad legs for many years. This condition started with bad veins, poor circulation and open sores. I believe it was or turned out to be diabetes. She eventually, by degree, had both legs removed below the knees. She had an artificial limb and supported the other knee on a chair, but she got around very well. She lived alone for about two years after John died; then neighbors Harvey and Marietta Brown moved in and took care of her. She died suddenly in June of 1924 at about age 70.

Elizabeth (Libby) Myers

Libby, my maternal grandmother, was born in 1856, the daughter of George (Miers) Myers and Nancy Somers, who lived in New York State about fifty miles west of Albany. She was one of eight children, four boys and four girls. They were quite a musical family. Libby could whistle about any tune that she was familiar with and sometimes would entertain at parties.

Her mother Nancy died at the age of just thirty-three leaving all eight children, ranging in age from about one and one-half through seventeen years.

During March 1867, their father George brought the family to Burton Township in Michigan.

Libby married Albert McTaggart. I think that his parents were from England. His brother Anson married Ida Shaw. One sister, Elizabeth, married John Goff and the other sister, Eliza, married Henry Smith. Eliza was my great-aunt and she gave me her ruby ring when I was about twelve years old. She could no longer wear it because of swelling in her hand. It is a beautiful ring and I still wear it sometimes. She and my mother were very close and she had no children of her own.

Albert left Libby not long before my mother Eva Gertrude was born on May 9, 1880. When Eva was about one year old, he returned unexpectedly and matter of factly asked, "Is this the kid?" At this time, Libby turned against him. He left and was never heard from again. His family remained very loyal to Libby who was a very hard working person and who raised Eva alone.

When Eva was about thirteen, Libby went to keep house for Frank Heermann whose wife had died and left him with four children all younger than Eva. Their names were William, Delbert, Mary Ann (Matie) and Louis.

Later Frank married Libby. They had two daughters, Alice Rhetta who was three years older than me and Lucy Belle who was one year older than me. During this time my mother Eva was married and I was born. I grew up with these two girls and since we always lived near each other we were about like sisters. It was probably good for all three of us, especially me, as we always had to share.

Frank was a farmer. In the early 1900's, he bought the forty acre farm where Ray and Beatrice Syring lived for many years. Harold and Wanda Dart now live in the house.

It was customary in those days to use the wagon or sleighs to take a load of produce to the City of Flint to sell on Main Street at the market area. There were many buyers there who bought right from the wagons. It was an all day trip. One day in about 1906, Frank made such a trip alone. On the way home, he had a stroke. The horses brought him home; horses were known to do that. He was quite helpless for about one and one-half years. Libby cared for him, which was a difficult task, and he died in 1908. After about three years, Libby sold the farm and bought a house in Swartz Creek where she lived the rest of her life.

Libby worked faithfully with the Ladies Aid Society in the Methodist Church as long as she was able. She was employed by the Swartz Creek Elevator for many years picking beans. This was done with a machine that was run by a treadle similar to the one on a sewing machine. The navy beans came down chutes onto a canvas belt and the women picked out dirt, small stones and badly colored beans as the clean white beans dropped into bins below. They were paid a few cents per pound for the waste that they removed.

Libby made hair switches from combings. All the ladies had long hair. The switches were about eighteen to twenty inches long. She washed and combed the hair and used it the same way as it grew. She sort of braided it onto a shoe string. It could be used in many ways to make a lady's hairdo very attractive. They wore very well and I still have mine after all these years.

I remember a few things that my grandmother Libby taught me:

MATERNAL GRANDMOTHER OF THE AUTHOR

Libby (Myers) Heermann. Photo taken at the time of her 90th birthday in 1946.

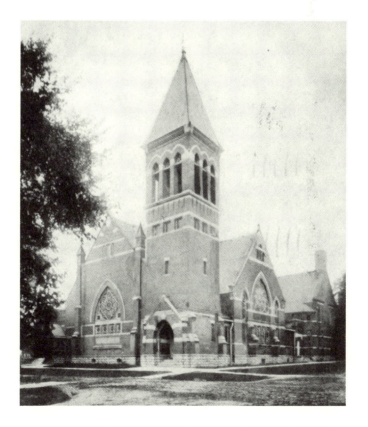

COURT ST. METHODIST CHURCH, FLINT, MICH.

Many people I knew were married in this church. It meant a train ride and a honeymoon in the big town.

WEDDING PICTURE

Frederick J. Knill Holland and Eva Gertrude McTaggart, 1899.

MY FIRST TWELVE
YEARS
1900–1912

My parents, Eva McTaggart and Fred Holland, grew up in the same neighborhood as teen-agers and attended the same social functions. They were married in 1899 at home by the Baptist minister.

The big industries in Flint during the early 1900's were lumbering and manufacturing wagons, carriages and carts. My father worked in one of these early factories. It was at the Durant-Dort Carriage Company in the paint department.

On March 8, 1900, I was born in Flint, Michigan, near the corner of 3rd Avenue and Smith Street which is now Grand Traverse Street.

In those days, many people felt it was a bad omen for a child to be left-handed. I think my parents were disappointed that I was, and they taught me to do many things with my right hand. Therefore, I am somewhat two-handed or ambidextrous. I do have a few problems, like deciding which hand to use, not knowing if I am turning such things as faucets on or off and not always

9

A FOURTH OF JULY PARADE

*Taken on Saginaw Street, Flint, 1900, showing three floats drawn by horses.
Fred Holland, father of Edna, is the first man on the left in a group of three
standing directly above the first letter "A" of the word CARRIAGE. The
sign on the side of the second float reads "Mfgs. of the Famous Blue Pigeon
Line."*

knowing immediately without stopping to think, which is right
and which is left. Maybe other left-handers have the same problem. As a child, I was sometimes called "a left-handed mossback"
and I really didn't care much for that!

In our family, we each had a nickname for as far back as I
can remember. Father's was Jimmy. I think that was because his
middle name was James. Mother's was Mike. I really don't know
why unless it was from the "Mc" from McTaggart. Mine was
Stub. I think that when starting to walk, I wasn't doing so well.
Dad booted me in the backside and said for me to quite stubbing
around. Stub followed me most of my life.

When I was about one year old, in 1901, my parents moved
to Swartz Creek, on the C.J. Miller farm on Morrish Road south
of Hill Road, where Leo Gilbert now lives. The old farm house
burned some years ago. Miller also owned and operated the

Swartz Creek Elevator and Lumberyard. My father worked the farm and helped some at the elevator.

About a year later in 1902, we moved onto the John L. Jennings farm on Hill Road at Jennings Road, where the grandson John Jennings now lives. Dad worked the farm for three years.

I can remember a few things while living there, like playing house under the porch with Gladys Jennings Bentley. Her brother Harry would ride me on his bicycle handlebars. That was big stuff. My mother and I would walk to the corner of Jennings Road to the mailbox. As we passed Henry and Grace Jennings' house, I would want to stop, expecting Grace to have something good for a handout. Kids always enjoy other people's food, even if it is the same as that at home.

In the spring of 1905, we moved to Cook Road, west of Linden Road. This farm was owned by William Peck. Mrs. Albert O'Connor now lives there.

My first memory of weddings is from that year. There were two that took place at the brides' homes. The first was when Floyd Robinson married Mary Myers. I saw some people in hidden corners sewing rice into hat linings and sewing up nightgowns and petticoats. I hadn't known about all those "monkeyshines!"

The second wedding that I remember was when Sam Day and Mary Ann (Matie) Heermann were married. It, too, was a home wedding. Tables were set everywhere. There was jello in little sherbet dishes, lots of people, excitement, and Alice and Belle Heermann and I trying to keep out of the way. I don't think that we did a very good job of it, but I was so fascinated by all the excitement.

We stayed on the Peck farm one year. In the spring of 1906, my parents bought the Shuman farm of Louise Shuman Williams. It is an eighty acre farm on the northeast corner of Morrish and Grand Blanc Roads and is now owned by Clifton Berlin.

I started attending the Fletcher School located on the southwest corner of Grand Blanc and Seymour Roads in September, 1906. I don't remember my first day of school, but I always enjoyed going to school. My parents kept me out of school for a while during the winter months the first year or so, because it was too far for me to walk alone. It did put me behind some which bothered me at the time, but my mother helped me with lessons and as time went on, maybe it was for the best.

I was about seven when I first remember experiencing death. We had some near neighbors who were close friends. They were Bert and Tina Hudson and they had one little girl Irene who was about three years old. I thought that I was a big girl when playing with her and taking care of her. One day she was playing with a mouth organ. A reed came out and she choked to death on it. I am grateful to my parents for allowing me to talk about it and to see her. It was a very sad time and I have always felt that I have had a better understanding of death because of the way that my parents handled it.

I didn't get into too much trouble as a child and I was embarrassed to have people know about it when I did. I could hold my own quite well. One day I wandered off with Cora Parks Todd without permission. Her hobby was finding four-leaf clovers, especially along the roadsides. I never knew anyone else who could find so many. When I arrived home — WELL!! I had to go to bed early without much supper. It happened that Cora's married sister, Marietta Brown, came in for a little while. The bedroom was close to where she was sitting, but I kept very still so she might not know where I was. Finally, she asked. My mother just said, 'She was tired and went to bed early." Thank goodness for my mother's little white lie!

In 1908, Jennie Myers Pratt, who was Libby's sister and my great aunt, went to the depot in Flint to take the train. While there, she had a stroke and died suddenly. She was in her early fifties. Her husband Orville Pratt had died some years earlier. They had no children. The seven other brothers and sisters lived to be elderly people. The Myers family divided her worldly goods. My mother was given her organ, the one that I now have. I was about ten years old at the time and I took music lessons on it from Fern Perry for a few years. She drove to the house in a horse and buggy. I think the lessons cost twenty-five cents each.

While walking to and from school, all sorts of things might happen. The most common would be getting your feet wet by falling into a rut or playing in the ditch. Two miles was about the farthest distance children had to go. Our Fletcher School usually

AN A.B. CHASE ORGAN

*Made in Norwalk, Ohio, during 1884, of hand-crafted black
walnut. It has a full six-octave keyboard which makes it a rare
instrument.*

had a large attendance so no one walked alone except if he happened to live at the edge of the school district.

One time the others were teasing me. I don't know what it
was about, but I guess that I got sick of it, so I said, "Shut your
clack." They got such a charge out of that, that from then on they

called me "Clack," especially my neighbors, Orrin and Lewis Rosenthal. I guess that I liked it as I never missed walking to school with them. They were big kids and I was little. They took such big steps that it was hard for me to keep up with them. I remember Lewis had good handwriting for a boy, one of the neatest I have ever seen.

I remember sometimes walking to the neighbors carrying a lantern to spend the evening. One evening in particular in the winter, we went as a family to visit Charley and Mae Rosenthal. Charley played the fiddle and tapped his foot to keep time. Mae played the pump organ. Orrin played the Jew's harp and was very good at it. I think they could have played all night and not stopped. Mae served popcorn which shut down the Jew's harp for a while.

My folks didn't give too many Christmas and birthday presents. Most of them were on the practical side but not always. I remember one Christmas my mother bought my dad an alarm clock. I think that they were quite new at that time. Mother read up on the instructions and set the alarm a wee bit early and put it behind the mantel clock, the one that I now have. Dad thought the mantel clock was ticking plenty loud, but I guess mother handled that part very well. I was in on the surprise. When the alarm rang in the morning, it scared the heck out of him. It is a wonder he didn't break some bones running around trying to find out what had happened, but he liked the new clock.

I learned how to do many things, for which I am grateful. I liked to write, draw and color pictures. Paper was scarce and I used every scrap not used for my lessons. I would cut it into pieces shaped somewhat like post cards and make my pictures according to the size of the paper.

Drawing and coloring pictures as a child was one of my favorite pastimes. People who lived nearby were very neighborly in those days. George and Belle Hunt were an elderly couple who lived close to us. They had no children. George's sister Sarah, a maiden lady, had come to spend her later years with them. Evidently, they liked the companionship of the children living in the neighborhood. I happened to be one of them and I thoroughly enjoyed this attention. Sarah was quite a good artist and she and I would draw and color pictures together. This was very helpful for

AUTHOR'S ART WORK AS A CHILD

Bersey Hull's Wedding - Cupid Firefighter - Putting cat in well - Lady in bustle

me. One time we entered a magazine drawing contest, but we didn't win anything.

I also liked to read. I especially liked "Pollyanna" and "Rebecca of Sunnybrook Farm." Years ago some educators decided that these books were not the best of literature. They felt they were too good to be true, but I think that they were good for me. I learned to be optimistic from reading these books. I believe that I have and still do accept disappointments very well. I usually take one thing at a time, don't get panicky, but find another way, making something work and just keep on going. Usually this has worked out for the best and always things could have been much worse.

My mother and I often worked out-of-doors helping with the farm work. I did about everything except plow and drill. Mother and I never did milk a cow. My father liked having me help him with most work rather than having a hired man. He trained me to do things the way he wanted them done.

By the time I was fourteen years old, I could handle a walking one-horse cultivator and a two-horse riding cultivator with which you had to be very careful in making the turn at the end of the row and not damage the crop. Also I could drive a team on the roller, the two-section drag, the spring-tooth harrow, and the dump and side delivery rakes.

The mowing machine and the grain binder, which my father also trusted me with, were a source of trouble because they were always getting plugged.

Loading hay and bundles of grain on the wagon in the field and driving the horses on the slings were other jobs that I did.

I walked barefoot behind a team of horses many a day, fitting ground for my father while he planted.

While my father was teaching me how to do the outdoor work, my mother was teaching me the art of homemaking. It seemed to me that it would be more interesting to be a good and capable wife for some eligible young man than to be a hired man. The household tasks that I liked were cooking, sewing, ironing, washing windows and cleaning the crystal and other doodads scattered about the house. I liked to see them sparkle and shine.

A job that didn't appeal to me as a child was "sprouting potatoes" in the springtime. People usually put more produce into the cellar in the fall than would be used, especially potatoes, as homemade bread and potatoes were our basic food and were usually served three times a day.

By spring the potatoes would start to grow (sprout). This would spoil the quality. The good food value would go into the sprout and the potato would wither and become less tasty, so it was necessary to remove those sprouts. The children were usually assigned this task. I didn't like it. The potatoes should be kept at their best for seed, market and for family use until the new crop came in about the Fourth of July. The pigs and chickens got the leftovers.

Our potato bin was in the dark part of the cellar near the big cistern. Water from the eave trough would sometimes drop into the cistern which would make a noisy splash! I would take a lantern and a little red chair into the bin. It was so still that I heard all of the sounds echoing around and couldn't see what was going on. It was somewhat frightening!

When we moved onto the Shuman farm in 1906, I became acquainted with the Parks family who lived across the road. I lived at that location until 1923. Beginning in 1906 and continuing until 1981, I have known seven generations of the Parks family. They are as follows, beginning with Henry and Marietta Parks who lived there at that time.

1. Henry and Marietta Parks
2. Norton and Nina Parks
3. Celia (Parks) and Garner Steele
4. Nina (Steele) and Albert Beers
5. Marla (Beers) and Gerald Sprague
6. William Sprague and Jyl Harrower
7. Jason Sprague and Sarah Sprague

I have always lived just a few miles from all of these people and have known six generations of both the Beers and the Steele families who married into the Parks family.

In those days people didn't go places too often. If they went very far, it took nearly all day. When going to Flint, we would drive three miles to Swartz Creek, put the horse in the hotel barn and walk back to the depot about one-half mile and take the train to the Flint Depot which was downtown. If we did not ride the train to Flint and drove a horse instead (or horses on the sleighs in the winter), we would put him in the ten-cent shed. We would take a little hay and a few oats and the stable boy would look after him until we returned.

The ten-cent shed had a waiting room with bench seats around the outside and a potbellied stove in the center. Some people would carry a lunch, others would buy things such as cinnamon rolls, bananas, cheese, crackers, etc. It was a nice place to meet people and visit. Some of the more affluent people would go across the street to the Dibble House and pay 25 cents for their dinner.

This Boutell ten-cent shed was later used for automobiles as well as horses. As time went on there were more cars and fewer horses, so the shed was razed and the Capital Theater built. It was and still is a beautiful building. For many years it was a popular and busy place.

My parents would usually travel to Flint one way and go back home another. This confused me, as I was afraid I would grow up and never know how to get to Flint and home again without getting lost.

Smith-Bridgman's in downtown Flint had a grocery store on one side of their building and a department store on the other. People would take their butter and eggs there to sell. Sometimes they would get a due bill and spend it in the dry goods part. I remember getting two coats that way; of course, only one at a time.

At that time, the Genesee County Fair was held the last of August each year out on Lapeer Road east of Flint. When we attended we carried our lunch. I believe it was about the same then as it was years later, with horse races, a carnival, exhibits and a merry-go-round.

The Pioneer Picnic was also held every year during the last of August, usually the third Thursday. Its location was on the north side of the road at McCann's Grove on Long Lake which is now Lake Fenton. Many people who attended were farmers. This was a convenient time of the year for them to get away because usually the oats were harvested by then and there was some free time.

The first picnic was held in 1857 and huge crowds came from great distances. In those early days, large boats on Long Lake carrying 300 to 400 people were kept very busy. People came from Detroit and other distant places for recreation as this was the largest inland lake in the area.

People took hay and oats for their horses and basket lunches for themselves. The food and dishes were spread on the ground on a tablecloth. The people sat on blankets on the ground. Sometimes a few families would share their food and eat together.

After dinner there would be speakers, probably political, followed by local entertainment. There would be boat rides, a ball game, a taffy pull, a merry-go-round and ocean wave. I really enjoyed these rides and have never seen an ocean wave any other place. As the ocean wave went around, one side went up as the other side went down. There were seats around the outside with a sort of canvas wall for protection. On the merry-go-round, we loved to ride the horses.

I have done some research to learn how these rides were operated in the early 1900's, but I haven't found anything or anyone who remembers. It could have been steam; if it was, the music could have been provided by a calliope, which had steam whistles and played by keys.

The taffy pull was a special event and interesting to watch as a man named Charlie Case made it. After cooking and cooling it "just right," he threw it over a large steel hook, similar to a fish hook, which had been placed in a tree. He worked it and pulled it over the hook until it was white and ready to snip. He made quite an exhibition of his taffy talent by attending the Michigan State Fair, County Fairs, and other gala occasions like parties for children at Halloween.

He made three flavors: vanilla, green peppermint and pink wintergreen. This was his recipe:

10 cups white sugar
5 cups Karo Syrup
7 1/2 cups water
7 1/2 teaspoons salt
10 teaspoons glycerin
10 tablespoons butter

Bring all ingredients to a boil. Boil until a ball forms in cold water. Cool. Work it with buttered hands and pull until white. Cut into small pieces.

We always attended family gatherings. The most regular one was with the Myers Family at Christmas. As time went on, these families became larger and the winter gatherings were not the best, so it was decided to have a summer reunion. I didn't know what a reunion was. It was decided to invite in other branches of the family which I didn't know existed. Now it would be the Myers-Somers-Griggs Reunion, usually held in August. The first one was held in 1911; Charles and Elizabeth Myers on Hill at Belsay Road, east of Grand Blanc, were hosts at their new house. These reunions were very well attended until 1980.

I always wanted to ride a bicycle and ice skate. There didn't seem to be a bicycle around for me to practice on, consequently, I never learned. I did learn to skate but not very well. Early skates were made to clamp on the soles of shoes. They were all the same and consequently did not fit on the narrower shoes of girls properly and were always coming off. Since I couldn't stand straight on them I think I must have had weak ankles. In later years, I had good shoe skates but I wasn't good on them either! Still, I always liked ice and snow. I was good at sliding on ice and sledding downhill and even enjoyed falling!

In those days we pumped water from open stone wells. These were three or four feet across and about twenty or thirty feet deep, depending on where the vein of water was. The sides were walled up with small stones; a platform was placed over the top and a hand pump installed.

Another type was a crock well. The crock was about 12" in diameter and about 20" long. The crock was bored into the ground, probably by horse power. Several other crocks were added on top of it, one by one, until the vein of water was reached. It also had a hand pump.

About 1908, my father hired Frank Lee from Linden to put a driven well down for us. A two-inch pipe was driven into the ground with a horse-driven winch. Lee kept urging the horse on with "Come on, Duke" and "Get along, Duke." It was a nice flowing well with water piped to the barn. From the tank, the overflow was ditched away so the barnyard was not muddy. The well was close to the house; however, it was not piped in, so we still had to carry water.

I don't remember going away to a Fourth of July celebration when I was young, but I always had about two packages of small firecrackers and some sparklers. To fire them, I had a long elder-berry stalk with a small hole in the end, just big enough to hold the firecracker. A pan of live coals from the cook stove was used to light them. This was bang-bang fun!

We usually made ice cream on the Fourth of July. We used milk, cream, eggs, sugar and vanilla. A freezer with a double paddle in the center of the can was turned with a crank. Around the can, we put cracked ice and coarse salt. The ice cream was frozen when the crank could not be turned anymore, the paddle was removed and everyone wanted to lick it.

The games we played were dominoes and flinch. Pedro cards were thought to be sinful in those days and were not allowed in good Christian households. "Hide the thimble" was enjoyed as well as, I guess, "Letter." The "it" person of the Letter game would think of an object in the room and tell us the letter it started with. Each person tried hard to guess it first so as to be "it" next time. Checkers was another popular game, but I don't remember that we played it much.

My father raised a few acres of alsike clover each year and sold the seed. It had to be handled with "gentle, loving care," so the seed would not shell out. After it was mowed, we would rake it with a dump or trip rake and put it into haycocks in the evening when it was damp with dew. Then later it would be drawn near to the barn and stacked to be threshed with a clover huller. It was usually a good money-making crop.

We had about an acre of cucumbers for a few years. The picking and sorting was a tedious job. The pickles were taken to Swartz Creek to the pickle factory, which was located about where Valley Petroleum Company is now. People were paid for them by the pound. The small cucumbers brought a much higher price than the large ones.

The mowing machine cutter bar knives, scythe, ax, etc. always needed to be sharpened and turning that grindstone was a

A JOB WELL DONE

Lester Green, left, and Fred Holland finish making cocks of alsike clover seed. Author Edna in the background on the seat of the dump rake holding the reins of the mare Daisy.

monotonous job for kids. I would think that we were about finished, when "No, just a little more!"

A similar task was turning the sheep shearing machine. Up until that time, shearing had been done with shears by hand. The machine had clippers and did a much neater and faster job. The wool was put into a threaded box and tied with wool twine into a fleece, weighing about ten to twelve pounds and then sold by the pound. It was supposed to look nice and be neatly tied. I could do a pretty good job of it.

On Sunday evenings, we often enjoyed my father's "special," a delicacy which he prepared. He scalded nice thick cream. To do this, the milk was placed in a "milk pan" for the cream to raise to the top. The pan would be put on the cook stove to heat until just below boiling when the cream wrinkled and was "just right." The cream would be skimmed off and served with brown sugar on a nice slice of homemade bread.

A few people in the area organized a Sunday School at the Fletcher School, which happened to have a pump organ. Some of

FARMYARD FROLIC

Left to right: Reba Kemp Parker, Bob Berlin and Alice Heermann Berlin. In the background at corner flowing stock tank, horse breaking carts with thills, carriage barn and livestock load chute.

the people who were the leaders were the Oren Bradys, George Blosses, James Lawthers, Alonza Coverts, the Perrys and Lilly Lawther. It was a success and continued for some time. I enjoyed it very much.

My father always had good-looking and well-trained horses. He took correspondence horse-training lessons from the Jesse Berry Horse Training School at Pleasant Hill located near Dayton, Ohio. I don't remember the number of lessons in the course, but he must have completed it. He and mother had a train trip to the school for about a week, as a reward. As a result, he trained many horses.

The Elie brothers, Lou and Floyd, in Rankin, did most of the horseshoeing and repairing of farm machinery, as well as setting the steel tires on buggies and wagons. The wheels were made of wood which would dry out and shrink. The steel rims would become loose and fall off if not repaired. The blacksmith would remove the rims, heat them, make them a little smaller by taking out a small piece to give them a very tight fit and put them back on. This would make the wheels last for quite a long while and then it would need to be done once again. The blacksmith used a forge to do his work. He would start his fire with kindling and use a special blacksmith's coal to heat the iron. To do the forging, there was a bellows attached to the firepot with which he could control the heat. The bellows was turned by hand. It required a very high temperature to heat the iron white hot. It was hard and muscular work and required a great deal of strength.

It was my job sometimes to go to the blacksmith to get these jobs done. Lou Elie, as long as he lived, would always tell me about the times that I went there and some of the things that happened. I guess that he was amused at the things that I was capable of doing.

Maybe my mother's misfortune was my good fortune. She had to do just the routine hard jobs that children do not like to do, instead of learning to do the more pleasant things. She had to scrub floors, which was a hard job at that time, wash dishes for at least seven people, dust, and clean until she hated all of it. She vowed that if she ever had daughters, she would let them learn other things. She kept her promise. I did the drudgery chores enough to know how and also learned how to do the tasks one likes to do.

My parents never made maple syrup, probably because we didn't have many hard maple trees. Oliver and Mary Dart, our neighbors, had a nice big sugar bush. It was a money-making crop for them. I happened to be around enough so that I had some knowledge of syrup making. The hard maple trees were tapped by boring a one-inch hole into the tree at the best working height. The hole was bored with a bit and brace about an inch or so into the tree. A spile was driven into the hole so the sap would run into a pail that was hung onto it. The sap was gathered, probably into barrels, pulled on a horse-drawn stone boat or pung to the sap house which was an open shed. It was poured into a large metal pan, maybe three to four feet wide, six to eight feet long, and six to eight inches high. The pan was placed over a fireplace to boil the sap to the right consistency. It takes about 40 gallons of the thin sweet sap to make one gallon of syrup. Sometimes someone would have to "sleep with it" to keep the fire burning and the sap from scorching. Some people "finished it off" on the cook stove in the kitchen.

There were different ways of cleansing it to make a clear syrup, such as putting milk or eggs in it and then letting it come to a boil and skimming out the impurities. Dart just let his syrup settle and left the settlings at the bottom of the container when he took the syrup off. I don't think that he heated it after it was at the right consistency. We thought his syrup was the best. Sometimes I got in on the "sugaring off." Mary made the best maple sugar; it was of a very fine texture. She put it in fancy small molds to make small candies to sell along with the syrup.

Sap runs the best when the temperature dips down below freezing during the nights and then thaws with nice, warm, sunshiny days.

My first automobile ride was with our neighbors, George, Lib, and Louis Eisentrager. Few people had cars at that time. We went near Flushing to visit some of their relatives who happened to also be friends of my parents. It was quite a thrill, sort of an "Oh and ah!"

Even though I was an only child, I was not alone too much. I was with Alice and Belle Heermann often. I also visited other friends and they visited me. I had a playhouse in a small upstairs room and a summer one under a big pear tree that was covered with grapevines in the back yard. It was so thick that the rain didn't come through unless it rained very hard.

I liked to go to Blair's, who were neighbors, to play. There were always many kids around at their house. It was sort of a meeting place. Addie Blair was the one nearest my age. She and I went through school together. We would eat carrots, green onions and rhubarb from their garden. I wonder that they had enough left for the family. Avery, Addie's father, would take a rest and read the paper at noon. The paper came in the mail before dinner in those days. Some people thought this was wasting time. As the years have gone by, I have decided that he was wise. I have found that I can work better after a rest.

In their woods was sort of a swamp where water would stand for a long period of time. It was large enough that George made a boat one time that would carry two people. When the water was high, he would row it around and take us for rides. We felt very adventuresome.

A short distance south of the Fletcher School, along the fence, was an apple tree on a farm belonging to John Quick. The school kids would shake the tree and knock down apples. Most of them had been to the tree at one time or another. One recess Addie and I, not being very big at the time, thought we would take our turn. I think about that time John decided to put a stop to it. He was laying in wait, for whomever might come next, with his horse whip in hand. We were scared stiff and never did get any apples. He didn't touch us; he probably couldn't get close enough as we were long gone. Maybe it was a good thing, as I have no desire to this day to pick anything along the roadside.

One time Alice and Belle Heermann and I were spending a few days with Charles, Lucy and Proctor Coates, our relatives who lived on Atherton Road in Burton Township. They had a croquet set which was a new game to me. I enjoyed it very much and hurried to play every chance I had. I went out on Sunday morning and had no sooner started playing than Uncle Charley, who was very religious, was there, too, informing me that we just didn't do things like that on Sunday.

The first remembrance I have of toilet paper was at the home of Uncle Dan and Aunt Anna Pratt, who operated a grocery store in Flint at the corner of East 5th Street and Lapeer Street. They lived in an old house next to the store. The privy was located at the back, in perhaps the woodshed. Being built on an incline, the drop underneath was a long distance down and light enough to see and watch the toilet paper unroll down the hole when started by some youngsters, one of them being me. The more it unrolled, the faster it went. It was exciting until we were discovered and the fun brought hastily to a halt. Before this, all that I had known about — was a catalogue!

The first real disaster that I remember was the sinking of the Titanic on April 14, 1912. It was the most luxurious ocean liner ever built up to that time. It was supposed to be unsinkable. People had been anxiously awaiting the maiden voyage from England to America with the wealthiest and most famous people in the world on board. The ship struck an iceberg at high speed and sank rapidly. About 1635 people perished; very few on board

DAN PRATT

In the milk peddling business. It was a training enterprise for the grocery business which followed.

This early photo was taken by "J. W. Applegate's Photograph & Tin Type Gallery" at the intersection of Perry and Gale Roads in the pioneer village of Atlas.

survived. Over the years, various groups of people have organized treasure hunts to locate the Titanic, but none have succeeded. In June of 1981, a man was interviewed on television who was well-organized and ready to make an attempt within the year. It was thought that if located, the wealth enclosed in the ship would exceed any amount ever recovered from a sunken ship.

In 1911, when I was eleven years old, Grandma Heermann thought it best to leave the farm so she sold it, the 40 acres, to Roy and Mary Burleson who became good friends of my parents. Their eight-year-old daughter Floy and I became acquainted and have been very close friends ever since.

HAYSTACK DOUBLING AS A CHICKEN COOP

LIFE
DURING THE EARLY 1900's

Telephones

Most new things were in the cities before they came into the rural areas. The telephone really had to be SOLD to the people. It would be costly, not necessary, and "Who would you talk to?"

About 1907 or 1908, Grand Blanc and Swartz Creek already had telephones. Some of the owners wanted to connect these two places by way of Rankin. The lines were privately owned. Some of the owners and promoters at the time were Charles Allen, Dee Lawrence and Ray Lee Gundry. To come through Rankin, the lines had to be put through using Grand Blanc Road and Morrish Road. People were contacted many times. These men believed in the telephone and had to use their salesmanship to convince the rural people to subscribe. If people didn't buy, they couldn't afford to build this connecting line. They persuaded enough people so that the line was built.

Subscribers were supposed to pay their bill every three months at the rate of $1.25 per month. There was a central office with people operating it around the clock. It was handled by plugs connecting the various lines.

The first operator in Swartz Creek was Mrs. Fred (Nellie) Fuller who ran the switchboard. She handled it in their drug and grocery store. They lived in the back part of the building. The telephone was made of wood, sort of box like, with two bells at the top and it hung on the wall. To call, you would turn a crank. There were several families on one line, each home having its own ring, which was a combination of long and short rings. Each call rang in everyone's home. That meant there were many nosy people listening in to learn someone else's business and gossip.

The poles didn't have arms at the top at that time to carry the wires as there were not that many lines. The wires were fastened to the poles with glass insulators. The roads were narrow and dirt with a single lane back then. There were plenty of small stones to throw at those glass insulators and that we did on the way home from school. I guess many were broken, much to the disgust of the telephone owners.

Lightning Rods

Lightning rods were installed on the roofs of most farm buildings and grounded in the earth. I think that insurance companies were the promoters. Many buildings have been burned when struck by lightning and many farm animals have been killed by lightning while standing too close to a wire fence or under a tree. Each lightning rod was equipped with a pretty colored glass ball. Nearly all homes had them installed. Later, roofs were capped with metal ridges. These were grounded thus doing away with the need for lightning rods. There are still some old-fashioned rods left on older buildings. My buildings still have the remains of them.

Peddlers

Peddlers traveled the countryside with heavy carrying cases and light trunks filled to running over with very pretty scarves, doilies, tablecloths, bedspreads and other items which they displayed by scattering over chairs. They walked great distances and I suppose, sometimes rented a horse and carriage from the livery stable in towns where they were working. Such trade was one way the livery stables earned their living as they owned many horses and carriages. It was a convenient service for people coming into town on the train. These peddlers were very persistent salesmen and we didn't always look forward to their visit, but they did often supply us with items that were otherwise hard to get.

Tramps

Down and out tramps came by often and would ask for handouts. Sometimes they would split wood or do some odd job to pay for some food and lodging. Maybe they would sleep in the barn, or on the porch, then walk on until the next night and find another place and do the same thing all over again. They traveled the countryside with their worldly goods in a bag on the end of a stick thrown over their shoulder. As the weather changed, they would hop a freight train and go to the part of the country that was comfortable. Many young men would spend a few years seeing the country in this manner, then settle down to a more useful life. For others, it was a lifetime career.

Gypsies

There were Gypsies who traveled the countryside in our area during the summer. There would be maybe four or five families, each in a covered wagon and with a few extra horses. They would camp along the roadside and stake the horses to feed on the grass. They made trinkets to sell or swap for horse feed and food for themselves. We didn't trust them and expected to have something missing during their stay — probably chickens. They seemed to have many children and dogs.

Farm Upkeep

Farm upkeep was done by hand labor with small tools. William Cupit was the wire-fence builder and a very good one in our area. He used cedar posts set about a rod (16½ feet) apart. A big post was set at the end and braced, then the wire fence was stretched with a hand stretcher to provide a very sturdy fence. Before this the fences were laid up with split rails in a zigzag way which made wide fence rows. It was hard work to keep them clean. The weeds had to be cut with a scythe. It was also a waste of land. Another kind of fence was a slat fence; the slats being held together with wires, however the slats were easily broken.

Drainage

Barney Hewitt was the best drainage man in our community. His services were booked in advance.

Land was drained by running branches of clay tile back from a farm outlet, which was usually a big open ditch. These branches were dug by shovel, spade, and a tile scoop which leveled the bottom on which the tile was laid. Barney was an expert at calculating the proper rate of fall required to move the excess water without the assist of a modern transit.

Farm drain tiles were made from clay. Frank Sharp, who lived southeast of us on the corner of Sharp and Ray Roads, had a tile yard stocked with tile he made from a clay pit on his own place. A six-inch tile, twelve inches long, was as large as he fired in his kiln. Sharp was an important country businessman.

Rhesa Alexander now owns and lives on that farm.

Painting

People kept their homes very neat. They pulled brush, cut weeds with a scythe, repaired their buildings as needed, and kept them well painted.

Houses were sometimes built with brick or stone, but wood siding was more commonly used and the roof was of cedar shingles. The painter who lived in Rankin at that time was Emile Simons. He was a big, strong man who could handle his ladders with ease and he used a big wide paint brush. At that time, there were no other materials used for siding except wood, so all wood houses had to be painted. People would often criticize Emile for painting on the comfortable side of the building, such as on the west side in the morning, the east side in the afternoon and catch the north and south sides at their best, which meant moving ladders often. I am sure that he could accomplish more by being as comfortable as possible. He could spread more paint in a given time than anyone else that I knew and without a doubt was quite wise to do it that way.

Barns

Many of the nice barns that were built in the early 1900's were built by John Lawrence, who also lived in Rankin. Those barns that were kept up are still standing.

Every farm had a woodlot. Timbers, rafters, and siding were all sawn from their own trees by a local sawmill. The carpenter would prepare the frame and rafters for the "barn raising" and then men and boys from miles around would come, as many as 50 or more, to raise by hand with ropes these timbers and rafters.

There would be a big "feed" in the yard on tables made of sawhorses with boards laid on top. Many relatives and friends came to help. Everyone, kids and all, came, as they had looked forward to a barn raising. These were special events during the summer.

Flypaper

Flies were a terrible problem especially where there were animals and barns. To get rid of them, we had sheets of sticky flypaper laying around everywhere with strips of it hanging from the ceiling. Fly swatters were made of folded newspaper. Sometimes the children would earn a few cents swatting them for a penny a dozen or more. That kind of chore could keep an enterprising child busy for hours.

Potato Bugs

Sprays for insect control were almost unheard of at that time, although Paris Green was sprayed on plants. Mostly, we "picked the potato bugs." This was usually the kids' job. We took a pan and a stick and knocked them into the pan. We poured a little kerosene over them to kill them or we dumped them into some hot coals from the cook stove. There seemed to be no end to those bugs.

Laundry

The wash tub was either galvanized or was made of wood and set on a bench or chair while in use. Some people would wring the clothes by hand, but most people had a hand-turning wringer clamped to the tub. Another tub was used to rinse the clothes, which contained bluing. This was a ball about the size of a marble. It was swished about until the water was the right color blue. This step was taken to keep the white clothes looking as white as possible.

Nearly all of the water used was soft rainwater. This was pumped with a hand pump from the cistern which might be located under a porch or in the cellar. It would be close to the kitchen sink. The people not having a cistern, which was walled up with stones or bricks and plastered so it did not leak, used a wooden rain barrel at a corner of the house to catch the water from the roof as it came down the eaves trough downspout. This caused mosquito problems.

The white clothes were boiled on the cook stove in a large galvanized or copper boiler. A copper boiler was more expensive, but well worth it if you could afford it because it would not rust and leak. The clothes were then lifted into the wash tub with a wooden stick and scrubbed on a wash board by hand with strong, probably homemade soap. After this they would be rinsed in the bluing water, wrung out, and the special clothes, such as shirt collars and cuffs and sometimes the fronts, petticoats, pillow shams (fancy covers for bed pillows that laid over the pillowcases), and other pretty things were starched quite stiff.

The starch was a white, odorless, tasteless, granular or powdery carbohydrate. It was moistened to remove any lumps, more water was added, it was cooked until smooth and clear, then thinned with more water depending on the stiffness desired. The garment was dipped into the solution, then wrung out. The clothes were then hung out-of-doors on a wire or rope clothes line with wooden clothespins to dry. Sunshine and a nice breeze made a perfect wash day.

In the winter, the clothes were hung around the house to dry. It might be the attic, porch, basement or on wooden clothes bars which would be set near the stove for faster drying.

Homemade Soap

Most of the soap used for laundry, cleaning and dishes was made at home. It could be soft and dipped out of a crock or hard and cut into cakes. The main ingredients used were lye, animal fat and water, which were all cooked together.

The lye was made by leaching wood ashes containing chiefly potassium carbonate. This was done by pouring water over the ashes and catching the liquid that drained through. This process might take several days. The fat was obtained at butchering time. The scraps and pieces not used in the household were "tried out" on the cook stove to separate the pieces and impurities from the good fat. There were proportions and cooking rules for the hard and soft soap. I think that it was a very strong soap. It was sort of an ugly brown color and had an awful smell!

Making Hay

Timothy hay was the main feed for the horses. It grows tall with a long seedy head and a small stalk with a few thin leaves. June clover was a better quality hay and was fed mainly to cattle and sheep. Hay was cut with a mowing machine which knocked down a five foot swath. The fence corners and other small places were cut with a scythe. People didn't waste anything that could be used. They also took pride in having neat homes and didn't let many weeds go to seed.

After being cut, a hay-tedder was used during the drying process to loosen and lift the hay to help it dry faster. Then it was raked into a windrow with a side delivery rake and loaded onto a wagon with a hay loader. Two or three sets of slings would be put in between layers of hay. These were made of ropes with cross sticks with a trip in the center. They were used to put the hay up in the mow in the barn. Along the ridge of the barn roof was a track and a car pulled by ropes and pulleys. The slings would be pulled to the top by horses and slid along the track to the proper place and tripped into the mow. A man with a pitchfork would pack it away. If there was too much hay, the extra would be put into a stack near the barn. If there should be more hay than needed, the surplus would be pressed into big bales sometime during the winter. A hay press would be set up on the barn floor. It would be powered by a steam engine. The crew would consist of six or eight men. One was the engineer. One hand fed the press. Two or three were required in the mow, depending on its size, to keep the hay a-rolling toward the baler. Two more were pushers and twisters. It took two men to stack the bales away because they were very large, weighing between 125 to 180 pounds.

Many of the men stayed all night and were given their meals. People had big houses and extra beds so this was not a problem.

Harvesting Grain

The grain, which consisted of wheat, oats and barley, was threshed in a similar manner. This was usually done in the summer. The grain was cut with a binder, with knives sliding back and forth, and dropped onto a table with a canvas drawing it up an elevator which made it into a bundle or sheaf and tied it with sisal twine. Usually the bundles fell onto a carrier which when full, with maybe four or five bundles, would be tripped to empty. This made it easier to collect into conical piles called shocks, which would end up scattered around the field. Sometimes, if the binder missed tying a sheaf, one would have to tie it by hand with a few stalks of grain in each hand to twist into sort of a knot and place the ends under the stalks to hold it in place. They held very well. My father taught me how to do this and I was good at it. It took a few days and required good weather before the bundles would be ready to put into the barn, stack, or to thresh from the field. At a later date, threshing directly from the field became possible as more threshing rigs appeared throughout the country.

The threshing was a big event and much hard work for the men as well as the womenfolk who prepared the delicious dinners and often suppers, too. The men soon learned where to get the best meals and took advantage of it. The word soon spread as to who were the best cooks and who put out the most food. Occasionally, there was not quite enough to go around and the last ones to the table were somewhat out of luck. No one wanted to be last. They were sure hungry and it was best to have plenty. It made for good gossip if someone didn't get fed! Then, there were a few people who would try to get out of feeding their threshers if possible, especially if they didn't have many acres of grain. They were soon caught up with and many pranks were pulled to stop and delay the work.

It took about a dozen men to feed the machine, carry the grain in bags to the granary, empty them into bins and to stack the straw. The straw was blown into the back barnyard. One or two men would place it into nicely shaped stacks to be used for bedding, feed, and many other uses. Some men took much pride in making a pretty stack that would not tip over or be ugly to look at. Some men were afraid to even try it. My father was very good at it. The horses and cows enjoyed running around the stack to rub their backs.

The threshing rig took three men to operate. One man tended the steam engine which was self-propelled at this time, and was quite new and modern. He fired it with mostly wood and maybe a little coal. The power was generated by the steam made by a boiler full of water. The water was hauled by a water boy with a tank wagon holding maybe 500 to 600 gallons which he pumped from a nearby pond or creek by hand. He used a fast team of horses and helped with other jobs when not hauling water. The separator man tended his machine and operated the straw blower. It took great skill for the engineer to place the separator and engine in the proper place and get the wide belt to run true so that everything worked properly. The fuel had to be fed into the firepot regularly to keep up the steam pressure. Too much steam could cause the boiler to blow up if the release valve did not operate properly. I knew a man named Otto Fulton, who lived in Clayton Township and married Fern Cole, who was killed by a steam engine when a young man.

Each engine had a pull whistle that was used when starting or stopping the machine or as a signal for danger. Each steam whistle had its own sound. Rigs could be recognized from as far away as their sound could be heard. I have always enjoyed listening to steam whistles.

Neighbor women and relatives helped each other with the meals and the dishes. It took a pile of towels that had to be washed by hand as well as all the dishes. All of the food was made from scratch and always homemade bread. Chickens had to be killed, dressed and cooked the day they were to be used, because there was no refrigeration and it was the usual main course.

All of the cooking was done on the wood range. The water was pumped by hand, carried in and heated in the teakettle or the attached reservoir that provided a ready supply of warm water. The men got very dirty threshing. Water was put out-of-doors in wash tubs that were set on benches or old chairs. The sun warmed it, and we put plenty of towels and soap nearby so everyone could wash at once before the meal began.

Navy Beans

Navy beans were a tricky crop to raise. If planted too early, they could be damaged by frost. If they matured too late, they might be damaged by the fall rains. They were pulled two rows at a time with a machine and raked into windrows and then forked into piles. When dried or cured just right, they would be hauled on a wagon into the barn or stacked nearby and threshed at a convenient time. It was a dusty and dirty job. The pods were used for rough feed for the stock, especially the sheep. In a good year, beans were a good money-making crop.

Sugar Beets

Sugar companies usually contracted the sugar beet acreage from the farmers. The sugar factories were located in Lansing, Owosso and Saginaw. This contract included seed and the help to block, weed, top and pile. This work was done with hand tools. The help was often people from the European countries, especially from Belgium, Hungary and Czechoslovakia. Whole families would work in the fields; sometimes babies would be born while the mothers were working there. They were a very hardy and hard working people. I think most of them were glad for the chance to get to America and stay, because they were good citizens, bought homes and prospered.

The beets were blocked or thinned while very small, one in a place, several inches apart to allow the beets to grow to an average of about five inches in diameter and several inches long. As they matured late in the fall, it might be very wet and muddy and this made the harvest difficult.

The beets would be drawn to a railroad station with a team and wagon, with possibly two or three tons on each load.

To determine the amount of dirt, leaves, etc., a man would take a sample of a few beets to determine the percentage of tare. The cleaner the beets, the better the price. The beets were handled with a large beet fork which had blunt tines that would not damage the beets.

While the beets were being harvested, they came in so fast that there would not be enough empty railroad cars, so they would be piled on the ground nearby. Later, after harvest, men who were not busy and had good sturdy wagons and good hauling horses, would put the beets onto the cars to be hauled to the sugar factories. It took strong muscles, a strong back and plenty of ambition to earn this extra money.

Some years the sugar content of the beets would be higher than others, depending on weather conditions.

Corn

Corn wasn't planted as thick nor did it grow as tall as it would in later years. Squash, pumpkins and melons were usually planted in the corn fields and grew very well. When planted with a hand planter, the field would be marked two ways, far enough apart to cultivate both ways. There would not be many weeds. A good crop should be "knee high by the Fourth of July."

Along in August, when the weather was dry and there was not much pasture, green corn would be cut each morning and thrown over the fence, usually into the lane. How the animals would come running to feast on it!

A few rows of late evergreen sweet corn sometimes would be planted in a handy place to be cut after the people had used what was wanted, as this came into use after the early garden sweet corn was gone.

When harvest time came, the corn was cut and tied into bundles which were shocked upright with about ten bundles in each shock. In a short time, the corn was dried well enough to husk with a husking peg which fit onto the hand to tear the husks away from the ear. The husked corn was thrown into a pile and the stalks retied into bundles and stood over the husked corn as another shock. When time and weather permitted, the farmer would draw the corn with the horses and wagon to the corn crib which would be near the barn. This crib was built up off the ground to keep mice and rats from getting to it first. The sides were made of slats with open spaces for plenty of air so the corn would keep dry and not mold.

The stalks, called fodder, made good inexpensive winter feed for cows, horses and sheep. The odd pieces which the animals couldn't eat made good bedding for them.

Crop of the Woodlot

Wood was the source of fuel and energy. Nearly every farm had a wood lot at the back end of the lane. Cutting wood was usually an all-winter job. The wood was cut a year before it would be used. Freshly cut wood was "green" and didn't burn very well. By the next year, it was "cured" and would burn nicely and throw off a lot of heat.

The trees were cut with a cross-cut saw with a thin blade which had a series of sharp teeth on the edge. To do a good job, the teeth should be sharp and "set" just so. Not all men could keep a saw in good condition. A few saws had one handle for one man to use but most of them had a handle at each end and required two men. This was easier work.

There was usually a sawmill nearby. The good logs were selected and drawn to the mill with horses over the snow on skids or sleighs. They were cut into various pieces of lumber to be used for buildings, gates, fences and many farm uses. Lumber and wood would sometimes be sold; it was another crop to earn much needed cash. People needed to be cautious not to oversell as it took about a generation for it to replace itself.

The tree branches and trees which had blown down were used for firewood. The large chunks were cut for the heating stove, which was a large round cast iron stove with a large door. These would burn for a long time if they were good hard wood such as oak, hickory and maple. This stove was usually placed in the living or dining room, depending on which room was the family gathering place.

The front part of the house was usually closed off for the winter. On special occasions, the parlor would be opened at which time it would be heated by a small sheet-iron stove. It would heat very quickly, burn out and cool off the same way.

The wood for the cook stove was split with an ax. Some kinds of wood split more easily than others. Ash was the best. The wood was cut about 18 inches in length, which fit nicely into all stoves.

Wood was sold by the cord which was a pile four feet high and eight feet long.

Some fence rails, smaller limbs and odd pieces would be

drawn to the back yard near the woodshed and cut when conven- ient with a bucksaw, which was a saw set in a frame. The wood pieces to be cut up were placed onto a sawbuck, which was a rack about knee high and 25 inches long with cross pieces at each end. These pieces were extended high enough to hold the wood. The sawyer held it in place with his knee, between the end cross pieces. He sawed it off outside of the frame.

Ice Harvest

I don't think that many people had an icebox, but nearly every farmer put up ice. Of the many uses for ice, I believe the main purpose was for freezing ice cream. It was a delicacy that we enjoyed often. We had all the ingredients and the only way to get it was to make it yourself.

The men would take the team and sleighs and go to a nearby pond or lake when the ice was ten or more inches thick. My father went to the Linden Mill Pond. The man who had the ice business for the village during the year would cut extra ice for the people who wanted it and charge for each block.

To cut the ice, he used a horse-drawn plow with a very sharp blade. He would cut about two-thirds of the way through the ice, then saw the rest of the way with a hand saw. The blocks would then float and were guided with a long-handled pike pole to the edge of the solid ice, and handled with ice tongs which were steel and very sharp on the end. As the handles were squeezed together, the tongs would grasp the block of ice which was about 18 inches square.

The ice house was usually a portion of some building not being used. Ours was part of a large woodshed which was parti- tioned off. Several inches of saw dust from a sawmill were put into the bottom. The ice blocks were put in and tightly packed and tightly sealed with ice chips to make a solid block. The top and sides were well covered with sawdust. As long as the air was kept out, the ice would not melt. To use it, a small part of the sawdust was removed. With an ax, one could chip out the size piece or pieces needed and cover tightly again with the insulating sawdust.

Domestic Animals

HORSES — Usually farmers owned three or four draft or heavy work horses and a light-weight driving horse. Many tasks required a three-horse hitch. Well-trained horses were very efficient workers. Many men were proud to test their horses in hauling heavy loads out of difficult places, especially at sugar beet harvest time, or to pull logs out of the woods, etc. The large collar that the horse wore was well padded and had to be a perfect fit to keep him from choking and prevent shoulder sores. The collar was where the heavy pull came from, as the driver held a firm and steady rein which was fastened to the bit (the part of the bridle held in the horse's mouth) to guide the horse. The heavy leather harness was kept oiled for protection and beauty. The brass buckles, rings and hames were well polished.

Teamsters were men who did various jobs, such as logging and building or repairing roads, or they could be hired for hauling crops after harvest or hauling wood to be sold. They were very good horsemen and needed good horses and equipment.

Some driving horses traveled quite fast, maybe eight to ten miles per hour. People enjoyed that when riding in their buggy or carriage, which might have one or two seats. Most carriages had a top over the seat that could be let down when the weather was nice. There were side curtains for stormy weather. They could be removed, rolled up and put under the seat. In front was a dashboard for protection against flying material picked up from the road by the horse's hooves. A whip socket with a whip to tickle the horse into a little more speed as you went zipping along was on the driver's side.

When a young man went courting, a whip socket was a handy place to anchor the reins if he had the urge to put his arms around his date. Also if he stayed out too late and went to sleep, the horse would take him safely back home.

In the winter, people used sleighs and cutters which were similar to a topless carriage with sleigh runners instead of wheels. To keep warm, we wore heavy clothing and we used blankets made mostly of buffalo, horse or cowhides. When we rode in the sleigh, the driver sat on a spring seat while the others sat in back in some straw. We used foot warmers such as soapstones or bricks which had been warmed on the kitchen cook stove.

Many city and village residents had small barns. They usually owned a cow, a few chickens, a horse, a carriage and maybe a cutter for winter travel.

COWS — The cows were just cows. They had not been bred to a size or shape, nor fed for high milk production. The production was somewhat seasonal. In the winter, they were fed hay, corn stalks and grist. This was ground grain, mostly oats and corn or barley. In the spring, they were turned into fresh green pasture. Later in the season when pasture was scant, fresh green corn was cut each day for them.

Some people in cities and villages had one cow for their own use. Farmers had maybe as many as three or four cows. They were put into the barn to be milked. They were fastened into wooden stanchions at the neck, tight enough to hold the head from slipping through. The milker sat on a one or three-legged stool to milk into a tin pail. The milk was carried to the house and strained through a fine sieve and a cloth. It was put into flat tin or granite pans about four or five inches high and about twelve inches in diameter. These were set on shelves in the pantry or buttery, in a cupboard with screen doors called a milk or pie safe, for a day or so until the cream would rise to the top so it could be skimmed off.

Another way to separate the cream was to use a water separator. This was a tin can holding about 15 gallons with a tapered bottom and a faucet. It set on legs high enough to draw the milk into a pail. About as much cold water was put into the can as there was milk. The cold water hastened the cream to the top. The watered milk would be drawn off, then the cream. The can would be washed and ready for the next milking. This milk would be fed to the pigs and chickens. The unwatered milk would be used by the family for making cottage cheese, cooking, etc.

The cottage cheese was made after the milk had soured and had become thick or clabbered. It was put on the back of the cook stove to warm enough for the whey to separate from the curd. The whey was drained off. When it was all drained and quite dry and firm, the curds would be seasoned with salt, pepper and enough milk or cream to give it the right consistency and taste.

The cream which was not used for cooking, whipping, ice cream, candy, etc. was churned into butter. It was usually sour.

One kind of churn for making butter was a tall crock with a dasher used to agitate the cream and was called a dash churn.

Another was a wooden barrel set in a frame and turned with a crank by a person sitting in a chair. As the barrel turned, the cream went swish, swash. As the chunks of butter formed, the sound changed to plunk, plunk. The liquid from the butter was buttermilk. This was drained off as much as possible. Some of it was used for cooking and drinking. The butter was put into a wooden bowl to be worked with a wooden ladle to get the liquid all out. Sometimes a yellow color was added to make it very attractive. It was put into crocks or various rolls or pats. The butter not used by the family was sold to customers and stores.

Heifer calves were kept to replenish the herd, while the bull calves were sold for veal at about six weeks of age.

Not many people butchered their own beef. It was hard to handle. There was no good way to preserve it. Occasionally, two or three families would share one. It would be butchered in the winter and hung in some outbuilding to freeze. A chunk would be sawed off for use as needed.

SHEEP — Nearly all farmers kept about twenty sheep to keep the farm neat and tidy. They kept the grass, weeds and brush trimmed around the buildings, fence corners, pasture fields, lanes and woodlots. They ate corn fodder, bean pods, etc. that the other animals didn't care for, but the lambs were fed enough better feed, such as hay and grain, to have them in good condition for market.

Sheep are sort of a helpless animal. If one gets down in a

hollowed out place, it is more apt to die than try to get up. Ewes usually have one or two lambs each year. Many times the ewe will disown her young; when this happens the lambs are bottle fed and end up becoming pet lambs.

Sheep produce two crops each year. They are sheared in the spring and the lambs are born in the spring and sold in the fall. Not all people care for lamb or mutton. It is a delicacy and usually brings a fancy price.

The wool is sold in the fleece and paid for by the pound which I explained in a previous chapter. Some people would take two or three of the best fleeces to a woolen mill to be made into batting to be used for comforters for beds. They are very warm and lightweight; real cozy. Garments made of wool are very nice to wear, but are not easily laundered. The fibers shrink very easily. It dry cleans nicely and is somewhat self cleaning.

As a money-making or sometimes a money-losing project, some farmers would buy a carload of 200 to 300 lambs shipped in by train from the grasslands of the west to feed through the winter with inexpensive feed, then fatten them the last few weeks before sending them to market.

When unloaded from the train, the sheep would be driven along the road by one or two men and a good dog to the farm which might be some miles away.

In the spring, they would be driven back to the railroad to be shipped to an eastern market, usually Buffalo, New York, hopefully for a fancy price to grace some well-to-do people's dining table.

HOGS — Pigs grow quite rapidly. There would be an average of five to eight pigs in a litter and two litters per year. They would be ready for market at about six to eight months of age at a little over 200 pounds each. Duroc Jersey breed was the most popular in our area.

Hogs were sort of garbage collectors. They were fed most anything that they would eat, but they were finished for slaughter on plenty of good corn. They were fed a grist made of oats and barley or corn. Yet another feed was "swill," a semi-liquid food composed of animal or vegetable refuse mixed with water, skimmed or sour milk, grist, garbage, etc.

Meat from hogs is called pork. The slaughtering or butchering was done at home in cold weather so the meat would cool properly, which was very important to retard spoilage.

A fire was built under a big iron kettle filled with water. When the water was hot the animal would be killed, allowed to bleed thoroughly, and then scalded in the hot water and the hair scraped off with a steel scraper. Poles were erected with a cross-piece on which the carcass was hung to be gutted and cut into parts that could be handled.

The entrails or innards were brought into the house and dumped onto the kitchen table which had been covered with newspapers. The organs, such as the heart, liver, tongue and kidneys, were removed. The pancreas or sweetbread was a delicacy. The fat stripped from the intestines was called "riddlings" and made into lard.

The leaf fat that was stripped from inside the rib area was the nicest and whitest and made the choicest lard. This fat was heated on the cook stove in big kettles. As it melted, the grease was poured off to cool and harden into lard. The crisp residue left from the rendering was called "cracklings." These with the rinds and a little shake of salt were yummy.

There seemed to be more ways of curing or preserving pork than other kinds of meat. One way was to smoke the hams and shoulders and make the side meat into bacon or salt pork. These pieces would be prepared by rubbing on a mixture of salt, saltpetre, honey, brown sugar, etc. or adding water and submerging the meat in the solution until it was seasoned properly. Saltpetre is a potassium nitrate rock salt which oozes from rocks and is used as a food preservative. At the proper time, the pieces of meat would be hung in a smaller building (smokehouse) on iron hooks over a slow-burning wood fire. Hickory and apple tree wood gave an especially good smoke flavor. It would go through this process until it was seasoned "just right" and until it would keep well.

Sometimes a tasty "pickle" was made with molasses, brown sugar, vinegar, salt, saltpetre, water, etc. The meat was placed into a wooden barrel or large crock and covered with the liquid.

"Salt pork" was placed into a brine strong enough to hold up an egg.

The meat placed into these two solutions needed to be freshened before cooking by soaking in fresh warm water.

Another way of preserving pork was to fry the slices of ham, chops, steaks and sausage until well done, and pack them into crocks, cover with melted lard and store in a cool place. This was my favorite way of preserving meat. It was especially tasty.

POULTRY — Nearly every home raised a few chickens. A few people raised some ducks, geese and turkeys. All types of poultry made for delicious eating, especially when there was no satisfactory means for cooking and preserving. Chicken was the quickest and the easiest to prepare and available at all times, for unexpected company or for the preacher for Sunday dinner.

An adult female chicken would lay about so many eggs and then get broody and steal away, make a hidden nest and if left alone, lay some more eggs, then incubate and hatch her brood. When possible, the lady of the house liked to arrange these settings in safe places, as rats and skunks and other small wild animals liked eggs very well, too.

A hen sometimes would sit on and hatch duck, goose or turkey eggs and tenderly care for these young the same as her own. She and her brood would be placed in a small wooden three-cornered coop with slats in front with feed and water. After a few days, the coop would be raised so they could come and go during the day but closed at night for protection, as many a stalking animal would find these tiny chicks a very delicious meal.

Hens didn't lay many eggs in the winter. It was impossible to have enough warm water for them. To have some eggs to use during the winter, which were quite limited and used mostly for cooking, they would be saved and placed into a container of oats and put in a cool area. They kept very well and would last until the hens started laying again when springtime rolled around.

The most popular breed of chicken was "Plymouth Rock," a black and white bird that was good for meat as well as eggs. They laid brown-shelled eggs.

Ducks and geese laid much larger eggs than chickens but not nearly as many and usually only in the spring of the year. Ducks and geese did better and enjoyed themselves more if a yard behind the barn contained a pond or stream.

Turkeys were tricky to raise but were often raised especially for the holiday festivities. They enjoyed roosting in high places and were difficult to capture and were always falling into something and drowning. We always considered them stupid.

Another product from the poultry was their feathers. The small and fine chicken and turkey feathers were used for cushions, pillows and feather beds. Duck and goose feathers and down were much nicer as they were fine, soft and lightweight. "Down" is a covering of soft fluffy feathers found on young birds and under the ordinary feathers of adult birds. This could be plucked from the adult birds during molting season without injury to the birds. It was hard to control as it was so light that it would fly all over the place.

Marketing

Grain was sold to the local elevator. Every town and city had one if it was located on a railroad line.

Hay was often hauled on wagons to the city of Flint and sold to buyers who handled their business on the open street corners.

Livestock was usually hauled to the stockyard in wagons or sleighs with high racks. Fat lambs or finished steers were sometimes driven but hogs — never. The railroads owned and maintained the yards which were located behind the elevator on a side track.

I remember two livestock buyers in Swartz Creek. They were Chris Skinner and the Carmichael Brothers, Ed, Albert and Bob. These men kept a keen eye on the market in Chicago, Detroit and Buffalo. They would visit the farmers in the area often to check on what and when their stock would be ready for market. There was competition between these buyers. As soon as a carload was bought, a day was set to bring them into the stockyard. The buyer had offered a price and would pay the seller on delivery. The buyer was in turn paid by the meat buyers in the cities.

Wagons and Bags

One kind of wagon had high wheels with narrow rims and a box about ten to twelve inches deep. The box could be removed and heavy two-inch planks about six inches wide placed on the bottom with ones about twelve inches wide standing on edge along the sides. This would be used for drawing manure when cleaning the stables and barnyard. When arriving in the field to unload the wagon, the side planks would be removed and the bottom ones tipped on edge. A curved, hooked fork was used to finish the job. It had all been loaded by hand with a shovel or fork.

This wagon was also used to haul gravel and other types of soil to maintain and improve the roads, which were under the supervision of the Highway Commissioner, who was a member of the Township Board. Nearly every farmer paid his road tax this way.

Another kind of wagon had lower wheels with wide rims. A wide flat rack was used on this one. When hauling livestock, either wagon could be used with board racks about four feet high. A chute with cleats was used to load the animals into the wagon. This one was used for hauling two to three tons of sugar beets to the railroad yards, for loading hay from the hay loader and hauling bundles of grain from the field.

The threshed grain and beans were mostly handled in bags. The grain bags were made of strong heavy off-white cotton and would hold about two bushels of grain. The men would balance them on their shoulders to carry them.

Everything was used until it was really worn out, so there was much mending and patching done mostly by the women. A much worn-out bag was used for patches. It might be done by hand or with the sewing machine. It was hard sewing; dusty, itchy and a very undesirable job. This was one of my jobs to help with when I was old enough and a real job after marriage. I never liked it!

Farms Needed Farmers

More people were earning their livelihood on farms than otherwise. There were not many big businesses to hire men. The land needed taming and people needed food and liked to eat!

The country had been divided into states, counties, and townships. Each township had been surveyed into areas six miles square, containing 36 square-mile sections. Each section had 640 acres of land and usually was divided into smaller parcels such as one-half section containing 320 acres down to one-sixteenth section containing 40 acres. This surveying pretty much determined the size of farms.

A good hired man was quite easy to come by. If hired for more than a few days, he would "live in," which would be part of his wages. An ambitious young man working for a good and prosperous farmer would be apprenticeship learning for his future. He would probably acquire a horse and carriage for his courting, save some money, get married, work a farm on shares, buy a team of horses, a few horse-drawn tools, a cow or two, a few chickens, a brood sow and start in business on his own. Soon he would buy a farm. Nearly everyone who did, paid for it and had a good and comfortable life.

Stores

GENERAL STORE — Stores in cities and towns were usually small and handled one line of merchandise. Individual merchants sold hardware, dry goods, furniture, meat, baked goods and so on and did not trespass on another storekeeper's business.

There were exceptions in sparsely settled areas such as Duffield and Rankin where there might be a church, school, blacksmith shop, and a general store which carried about everything from toothpicks to horse collars. The telephone operator (central) might be located in a corner of the store along with the post office.

There would be a large wood-burning pot-bellied stove near the center of the store with a few chairs and a big spittoon or cuspidor nearby. This could be a "hang-out" for men to "get away from home" to learn the news and gossip. This was looked forward to and enjoyed.

Items were not prepackaged. Nearly everything came in large quantities in barrels, boxes, or cans to be cut, sliced or dipped into for the amount wanted. All items were handled over a substantial wide counter. There would be a coffee grinder with great red wheels and a big handle which was turned by hand.

A large round cheese under a glass cover was on the counter and would be cut to any size wedge wanted. Each item was put into a brown paper bag or wrapped in wide paper that was pulled from a roll to the size needed and torn off, then tied with cord or string which was pulled from a big spool which hung from the ceiling and cut to the right length to tie the package. Upon arrival home, the items bought were put away, the paper and sacks were folded carefully and put in a handy place. The string or cord was wound onto a ball. These were used in various ways around the household. This was something we didn't have to buy since we saved as much as possible to be reused.

The store handled a few pieces of material and sewing notions, many farm supplies such as plow points, cultivator teeth, parts for harnesses, ropes, hoes and shovels. You name it, the general store had it, and people liked that.

SALOONS — The saloon served only men. Some were "hardcore" drinkers. Men who were moderate and just liked to take a nip now and then would occasionally sneak in but they didn't like to be seen entering, as their friends might have the wrong impression of a "good man." The saloon in Swartz Creek was located near the corner of Morrish and Miller Roads, where Ketzler's Too Flower Shop is now located.

At the time, all of the people in town walked to the Methodist Church and had to pass the saloon. It was very objectionable and offensive. They just wished it wasn't there.

The Reverend E. H. Wilcox was the minister at one time and being a friendly chap, as he passed by the saloon, he stepped to the door and called out, "Good morning."

Not realizing who it was, Homer Wade called out, "Go to hell!" Then soon discovering his mistake, apologized and apologized.

Reverend Wilcox calmly answered, "You might as well tell *me* to go to hell as Horace Bristol."

GROCERY WAGON — The person operating a country store would sometimes operate "Grocery Wagon" weekly routes while someone in the family or a hired clerk watched the store. He drove a team of horses hitched to a covered wagon made of wood with shelves and several different sized doors. One big door would let down to form a counter. He had his scales with him to weigh the items as they were not prepackaged.

Minor Snow of Duffield came to our house. Mother usually bought something from him as he carried many necessary household items.

He would arrive at the Fletcher School at about first recess. If he was late, the teacher would let the pupils be excused to make their purchases, which were usually gum, licorice, horehound, peppermint stick, pencils, crayons or tablets. My parents didn't let me buy. I guess I thought I was badly abused. Later I thought it was a good idea that I didn't have to buy something just because it was available.

DEPARTMENT STORES — Department stores were usually very nice and had about three floors. I remember a few in Flint: O.M. Smith, Warrick, Hill Bros., Bridgman, and Herbert N. Bush.

The clerks did the selling but handled no money. When paying for the merchandise, each department had a station. The money and sales slip would be put into a small container or car which had little wheels. This would be fitted onto a wire track. To release it, a cord would be pulled and it would take off at great speed near the ceiling to the office, which was usually located on the mezzanine floor. This was a small glassed-in room with a good view of the main floor. I think that was a security measure to catch any "would be" hanky panky.

The business, change and receipt would be properly attended to. The car would be placed back on the track for a speedy return trip. It was fascinating to me to watch as a child.

This contraption must have been powered by the store with their own electric generator as there were no electric power lines at that time.

Trains

The railroad played a very important part in developing the United States and contributing to its progress. In the early 1900's, the railroads were in all parts of the United States and were flourishing. They were powered by coal-burning steam engines which were operated by the engineer and fireman.

Durand was the "railroad center" in the area where I lived. Many lines crossed at this place from all directions. This depot was the largest one for many miles around. Many people and their baggage came through Durand every day. There was also a large "round house" that could house several of the huge "iron horses" to be checked, repaired or put on the road when needed.

Shipping by waterway was also big business. The railroad connected with the waterways which made for very efficient transportation.

The railroad made travelling possible for people on either long or short journeys. A very luxurious trip could be had by paying extra. There were diners and sleepers with attendants to serve one's every need and whim. These cars were finished with beautiful wood, such as mahogany, and lovely upholstery. The conductor wore an attractive uniform and cap. He took the tickets, answered questions and looked after the passengers in general and was a very important part of the railway system.

At this time, the roadsides and tracks, which were owned by a "railroad company," were kept immaculate. The working men reached their working area by handcar. The men carried their tools and powered the car by hand. Each car carried about four men down the tracks. This car would be lifted off the track while trains were passing. The brush and grass were kept trimmed and cut with hand tools such as saws, axes and scythes.

Interurban

The interurban that I am writing about is an electric railroad which ran from Saginaw to Detroit from 1901 to 1931. Some of the towns and cities that I remember this one-car vehicle going through were: Flint, Goodrich, Ortonville, Lake Orion, Pontiac and Rochester. There were local and express cars which ran about every two hours. The local car stopped at nearly all highway or road crossings. The express stopped only at cities and villages. There would be at many crossings a small building that served as a waiting room for weather protection. People would "flag" down the interurban, be picked up and on they would go. It was a one-man operated car. It was an affordable way to travel.

Health–Illness–Remedies

Hospitals were few and far apart. I can remember Hurley in Flint and Wheelock in Goodrich. They were miles away and there was no comfortable way for a sick person to get there.

The country doctors in the small towns were general practitioners who treated people in their offices if they were able to come. Those who were too ill, the doctor would visit at home,

INTERURBAN

On the main line south of Flint.

sometimes driving his horse and carriage many miles. All babies were delivered at home with the doctor and mid-wife (perhaps a neighbor lady or a relative) in attendance. The doctor would carry with him in his little black bag, the instruments and medicines that he needed.

Some of the common adult diseases were: tuberculosis, then called consumption; stroke, often called apoplexy; and pneumonia.

Children's diseases were: croup, whopping cough, mumps, red measles, German measles, and scarlet fever. Some of these contagious diseases called for a quarantine. People could neither come nor go. Someone would bring in supplies. A big sign would be put in a sightly place to keep people out. This would go on for several weeks, until you were sure that no more members of the family would come down with it. As soon as the sign was removed, everything in the house had to be washed in very hot water and very strong soap and the house was thoroughly aired.

Some home remedies were:

Goose grease and, I think, turpentine saturated on a cloth around the neck.

Mustard plaster on the chest.

Watkins liniment, internal and external.

Hill Bros. Cough Drops.

Camphor; quinine (very bitter).

Sulphur and molasses.

Teas brewed from many weeds.

Epsom salt, internal and external. Epsom salt dissolved in very warm water was used to soak bruised or swollen parts of the body.

Chilblain was another common condition. It was a blain or inflammatory swelling, due to freezing or exposure of the feet, hands, ears or nose. People's toes were especially affected. It was hard to keep one's feet warm. It seemed like they were cold all winter. We had warm stockings and overshoes, but the floors were always cold. A stove didn't warm floors, no matter where we went. Even with our warm bricks, stones, flatirons or soap-stones, our feet didn't stay warm in very cold weather.

Funerals

Everyone *must* wear something black to a funeral. It was disrespectful and rude not to display some kind of mourning, such as a black crepe arm band, hat band, tie, dress, suit or lady's veil.

Mourning for family members went on for some time, from six months to a year.

The corpse was always kept at the house where the visitation took place. Some relatives or friends always stayed all night and would sit up all night so the family would not be left alone.

A wreath was placed on the front door to inform people that there had been a death in the household. The funeral was held at the home. The black hearse was drawn by a span of horses, often black ones, wearing nicely oiled harnesses. The mourners followed with their horses and carriages all shining and clean. All traffic must stop and the men doffed or removed their hats as the procession passed. People were saddened if the procession traveled too fast.

Rural School

The schoolhouse had one room, one teacher and a room full of children, maybe as many as forty in grades first through eighth. Older children who had already finished school would come back through the winter when there wasn't much work to be done at home. Many never went to high school. People didn't think it was necessary. High schools were few and far between and transportation was difficult to arrange. Sometimes students lived in town and boarded with friends or relatives.

The teacher had to be master of all trades and he or she would usually board and room in the area. If a child was hurt or sick at school, it was handled there. There was no telephone at the school and there was no transportation available to the teacher during the school day.

The boys' wraps and dinner pails were on one side of the room and the girls' on the other. The outhouses or privys were arranged the same way with the woodshed in between.

The potbellied wood-burning stove might be placed anywhere and get the room warm by late in the day. Sometimes the teacher would hire one of the older boys to build the fire and do some sweeping.

The small seats and desks were in front and graduated to the big seats in back. Usually they were double seats, so we sat with someone. The back seats had ink wells. Some of the pupils had ink bottles. It was always being spilled. What a mess! It always left a stain. In cold weather the ink would freeze. We used a steel pen point attached to a handle and wrote on very smooth paper. When the point didn't work well, it could be changed. For our lead pencils, we had rough paper.

Everyone had a slate and a slate pencil or chalk. This was quite sloppy to erase and wash, but it was very economical.

There were blackboards on all sides of the room. Few were slate, which was the best and the most costly. Fletcher School had a composition board which was green. Chalk was used for writing on these boards.

In the front of the room, near the teacher's desk, was a long recitation seat. All classes recited there. Sometimes if a boy liked a certain girl, he would maneuver to sit beside her during class.

A large dictionary was usually placed on a shelf in sight of the teacher so that its use could be monitored by the teacher.

Schools were located so no one was supposed to walk over two miles. Parents very seldom took their children to school. We wore warm clothing and wallowed snowbanks, mud and jumped creeks to get there.

School sessions were from nine to four with two fifteen minute recesses and one hour for noon, from September through May.

We carried either tin or granite lunch pails. I don't know if other schools did what we did or not, but if something was left from lunch, at the last recess, we would swap. Other people's food was a treat. We soon learned whose mothers were the best cooks.

We usually had a morning exercise that consisted of one of the following: the teacher reading to us, having us give a quotation or group singing. We played blackboard games, such as Dot and Old Cat or Tic Tac Toe.

Outdoors we played Tag, Dog and Deer, Foot Race, Duck on the Rock, Anti Over the Woodshed, and ball. I liked to play ball. We would choose sides, both boys and girls. There was not enough of either to make two teams—it took all of us!

The Tibbits children had a big sturdy sled made of sleigh runners. Two husky boys or girls would pull it with a rope, filled with as many as possible hanging on in all directions, going around the schoolhouse as fast as they could go. By the time they had gone around once, nobody was left on. They were strewn all over the place and what fun!

It was fun to "hook a ride" on the sleighs and cutters when people were passing the schoolhouse. Some men would "lick up the horses" to see the kids go tumbling off.

By the time we had finished grade school, we would have studied reading, writing from a copy book, arithmetic, orthography (now called phonics), geography, physiology (now called health), history, grammar, civil government and spelling.

The interesting thing about spelling was "leaving off head." We would stand in line and each have a number. The words would be pronounced from the head to the foot of the line. When a word was misspelled, the next person to spell it correctly would pass the person or persons who misspelled it. The object was to get to the head. You would get your mark, then go to the foot of the class and work your way to the head again. How we would work to see who could get the most marks or "leave off head" the most times! It was a good way to get good spellers.

When finishing the grade school, one had to pass the eighth grade examination to be eligible to enter high school. This examination was put on by the state and held at a nearby high school, under the supervision of the superintendent. It took two days. Those who passed the examination went to the County Court House for graduation and to receive diplomas.

In May on some nice warm day, everyone in the one-room country school would go to some nearby woods to pick wild-flowers, such as violets, mayflowers, adder's tongues, jack-in-the-pulpits and trilliums.

The last day of the school year was usually a picnic when the whole neighborhood would come.

Fletcher High School

Since Fletcher School had always been large, about 1910 some people in the community thought it should become a high school. The district was divided on this issue, so it was decided a vote would be taken. Everyone eligible to vote was brought out. At this time, some men didn't believe women should have many rights, so women had to own property to vote. I remember one man who was so opposed to the idea of Fletcher School becoming a high school that he gave his wife a joint deed to the back forty so he could have one more vote. All he cared about was another vote in his favor; he was obviously not real interested in sharing his landholdings with her. It was good that the proposal was defeated because the area was too close to Gaines and Swartz Creek for another school, but the issue was very heated and for some the wounds remained for life.

Wells and Water

Many wells at schools and homes were "open" crock or stone about three to four feet across and twenty to thirty feet deep. Water seeped into the pit from the outside and from rain. They were covered with heavy boards. Water was pumped up with a hand pump. Someone would pump a pailful, take it into the schoolhouse or kitchen, set it on a shelf or table and there would be a long-handled dipper in the pail for drinking or filling the teakettle.

Some wells were near the barn for watering the animals. Water was not wasted because it was too hard to come by. Wash water from the laundry and dishes and baths was used for watering gardens, flowers and scrubbing floors, porches and the outhouse!

Berries

Rural and small town people raised most of their own food. This included fruit, grapes, berries and nuts. They raised strawberries and raspberries in the garden.

They gathered many wild berries, such as blackcaps, black-berries, elderberries and wild strawberries which grew along fence rows and in the woods. Huckleberries grew wild in swamps which were located on some people's farms. In our area, some of these farms were located near Argentine. These berries were ripe at a slack time in farming during July and August. A few families would arrange a picnic dinner to go "huckleberrying." They needed to wear rubber boots to protect them from snakes, deep water, etc. The owner would charge a fee for each person or perhaps for a family. Some people were excellent pickers and obtained many lovely berries for a reasonable price as well as having an enjoyable day.

Grapes

Nearly everyone had a few grapevines, usually Blue Concord. These were especially good for eating, juice and jelly. Jelly was made mostly "by guess and by gosh," which meant so much juice and so much sugar, probably equal amounts, boiled until it "leather aproned" off the spoon. It might have to be boiled again as it might be too soft or too hard and rubbery. There was no such thing as Certo or Sure-Jell then.

There might be a few peach, plum, cherry and pear trees. These were somewhat short-lived except maybe the Bartlett Pear.

Nuts

People didn't buy nuts, except peanuts, and they are not really nuts as they are grown in the ground. Real nuts grow on bushes or trees. Hickory nuts, black walnuts and butternuts grew in the woods, fence rows and roadsides. Cracking and picking out nutmeats was an evening and family operation. Hickory nut cake and candy were delicacies.

Apples

The apple orchard was the largest of the orchards and the most important. These trees lived for many years, grew very large and produced much fruit.

There must not have been as many hungry worms and insects at that time as we raised nice fruit and knew nothing about sprays.

There were many varieties of apples. Some that I remember were: Transparent, Sheepnose, Baldwin, Western Stripe, Duchess, Snow, Northern Spy, Tolman Sweet, Greening, Maiden Blush, Russet, and Pippin.

We had apples nearly the year around. They were placed on racks in the cellar and would keep into the springtime. The cellar, which had no heat and enough dampness, would keep the apples firm and fresh like.

I remember my parents selling some Northern Spys in the spring to the store and they in turn sold them for five cents each while my parents were still in the store. I don't remember how much my folks received for a bushel, but I think it was a very good price.

The Russet was best in the spring after it had been placed in a pit in the fall. This pit was a hole in the ground near the garden with some straw added, and whatever produce one desired to place into it, such as apples, turnips, rutabagas, carrots, potatoes, etc. They were covered with boards and coarse manure. These items should be used as soon as possible after being removed from the pit, as they wouldn't keep long. That was the reason for removing a few at a time.

Cider

In the fall after the best apples had been picked and put in the cellar, the next best ones were loaded onto the wagon along with barrels and kegs to be taken to the cider mill. The juice would be pressed out. The pulp would sometimes be brought home and spread on the fields or fed to the livestock. If the pulp had been around for a few warm days, the pigs might get a little tipsy.

The cider barrels would be placed in the cellar, using planks and ropes to ease them down the steps which might be an outside cellar way.

Cider would stay sweet for about two weeks, depending on the weather. It gradually fermented, becoming hard cider, then it turned to vinegar.

Hard cider was perhaps the most popular alcoholic drink for those who enjoyed imbibing. It was very inexpensive and easily obtained. Some people doctored it up some by adding raisins, corn or wheat, etc. to retain a good taste so it would be pleasing to the palate and keep it from turning to vinegar. It didn't take much to make a man tipsy. Most ladies didn't drink intoxicating beverages. It wasn't ladylike.

Tom Penny fixed his barrel really good and tightly sealed it. He called it his "June barrel." He had a special opening, and invited his friends, lawyers, judges, the sheriff and politicians to his "Grand Opening!"

Houses

Most houses were large and well-built. Material was plentiful and inexpensive. Carpenters were proud of their workmanship, and they were not pressured for time.

The ceilings might be ten to twelve feet high. The walls were lath and a coarse, crumbly hair plaster. This required wallpaper. The border was usually eighteen inches wide.

The bedrooms were very small and the closets were tiny or not there at all. The other rooms were large. Some extra rooms would be closed during the winter as they were difficult to heat with stoves. The stoves would be removed during the summer and freshly "blacked" with stove blacking when put up in the fall.

The parlor was just used on special occasions. It must be kept in tip-top shape for funerals, weddings, special entertaining and courting. It probably looked like this: ingrain carpet, a small sheet-iron stove, a pump organ, a plush velvet covered love seat, and one or two matching chairs, a marble top table and enlarged pictures of Grandpa and Grandma in elaborate frames hanging on the wall. There might be an unused fireplace.

The other rooms would have rag carpet and rag throw rugs. These were made of old garments torn into strips, sewed together, wound into balls and taken to someone who had a loom threaded with heavy warp and woven into strips the length of the room. The strips were then sewed together. The floor was covered with papers or straw for padding. The carpet was stretched and tacked around the edge of the room.

Occasionally, it was taken up and hung over the outdoor clothesline on a windy day. It would be vigorously beaten with a wire carpet beater. How the dust would fly! It would be put down again on a clean floor and new padding.

The kitchen floor might be wide boards with no covering. This required down on the knees scrubbing.

The wood-burning cook stove had a reservoir attached that was used for warming the soft cistern rainwater that was preferred for washing clothes. This water was not used for cooking or drinking. The cast-iron sink had a pitcher pump for pumping water up from the cistern. There might be a large pail setting under the sink if there was no drain to the outside from the sink. This had to be emptied frequently, sometimes on the garden.

The buttery or pantry was a small room off the kitchen. It had shelves and cupboards for storing all of the ingredients for baking, dairy products, the cooking and serving dishes and a work table for mixing, kneading and rolling all the goodies on baking day.

Dinner Bell

Nearly every farm had a large bell hanging in a belfry, usually on the roof of the woodshed or on a tall pole nearby. Pulling a rope would ring the bell, which could be heard for a great distance. A bell was necessary for farmers since not all men carried watches. Bells could be heard all around the countryside at dinner and supper time. The horses knew the meaning too. They would "hurry" when headed toward the barn at this time.

The bell was also a great help if something should go wrong at any time.

Linens

A checkered cotton tablecloth or oilcloth was used on the kitchen table for everyday use.

When company was expected, a fabric tablecloth was used. Damask linen was often used. The direction in which the threads are woven creates a distinct pattern on this one colored material. Usually it had a floral motif and it made beautiful tablecloths and napkins. They were hand hemmed along all the edges. When they were used, a beautiful table was set using all the best china, crystal and silverware.

Doilies, dresser scarves and other things were made of fine linen with various kinds of lace trim.

Bedding

Muslin, a somewhat heavy cotton cloth, had many household uses. It was used especially for sheets and pillowcases and could be bought either bleached which would be white in color or unbleached which was more of an ecru color. Unbleached was less expensive and was supposed to wear longer. After many washings it, too, became white. This material was 36 inches wide as were most materials, although a few were only 27 inches wide.

To make sheets, two widths about 84 inches long were sewn together by hand and hemmed along the ends. The pillowcases were 27 inches long and were sewn across the bottom and along one side.

Quilts were made from left over pieces from other sewing, and contained a cotton batting or occasionally a wool bat. They needed to be warm. There were but few blankets to be had and "they cost money." In the winter we did use outing flannel blankets. They were very cozy.

The straw ticks, feather beds and skimpy springs made a smaller bed, so the bedding could be smaller. This made for easier handling when using hand labor for laundering.

Towels

When wheat was taken to the mill and exchanged for flour, both bread and pastry, it came in 100 pound cotton bags. The farmers who raised sugar beets also got their sugar in 100 pound cotton bags. All these bags were washed and hemmed and made into nice dish towels. In fact most of the towels belonging to farm families were made from cotton sacks.

The nicest towels were made at home from Stevens linen crash which was bought by the yard.

Wash cloths, dish cloths and scrub cloths were made from worn-out knit underwear.

Food Drying

Drying was a means of preserving many kinds of fruit and vegetables. My mother dried apples and sweet corn.

The corn was cut from the cob and placed in thin layers on flat pans on the back of the stove and stirred frequently until very dry and stored in a covered container. To use, it would be reconstituted by soaking in water for a few days, then cooked. It was delicious.

The apples were pared and cut into thin slices, dried and handled the same way as the corn.

My mother made a dried apple cake with hickory nuts in it. It was our holiday cake, and it kept very well providing we didn't eat it too fast.

Mincemeat

There seemed to be three basic ingredients needed for good mincemeat. It would usually be made after butchering when meat would be available, along with apples and raisins. Other ingredients were spices, sugar, cider or vinegar, and maybe some other fruits. This would be cooked and ground and seasoned to "just right" and then canned.

Yeast Starter

It seems that to make bread and pancakes, one had to use a "starter." I don't know if the yeast was slower rising at that time or if people didn't want to wait.

I remember my mother using the starter. The problem with this is — once started, it should be used regularly, about twice a week or oftener to keep it from spoiling. Some people would run out of starter and borrow from a neighbor.

As I remember, yeast was somewhat coarse and crumbly. This is about the way the starter was made: Cornmeal, hops, warm water and maybe a little sugar were mixed together. The sugar was added only to hasten the fermentation. It would be bubbly and give off a sour smell.

Hops

Hops is a twining, rough-leaved vine, planted in hills. Each hill requires a pole, ten to eighteen feet high, to support the vine. Hops are cultivated for their loose, papery, fragrant catkins for use in brewing beer. The valuable part of hops is the bitter principal. It contains a granular powder on the scales and the inner shell of the tiny seed is utilized to flavor the yeast. Hop yeast is the best for raising bread.

Lillian Eddy, whose husband was pastor at our church for a number of years and retired in our neighborhood, gave me the following recipe. It might be called "Sourdough" now.

Old-Fashioned Buckwheat Cakes

1 quart warm water	2 tablespoons sugar
1 cake dry or compressed yeast	1 cup sour milk or buttermilk
1 cup yellow cornmeal	1 teaspoon salt
4 cups buckwheat flour	1 teaspoon soda

Place warm water and yeast into large mixing bowl and soften yeast.

Add cornmeal, buckwheat flour, sugar, salt and buttermilk. Beat until a smooth batter is formed. Cover and let stand at room temperature overnight.

In the morning, add the one teaspoon of soda dissolved in one-fourth cup of warm water. Mix and bake on hot griddle.

At least one pint of the mixture should be saved for a starter for the cakes the next morning.

In the evening, add ingredients with the exception of the yeast and soda, then again set to rise. In the morning, add the soda as before.

Watkins Products

The Watkins salesman had a territory which took a few weeks to cover by driving his horse and buggy, door to door. He would then repeat the area so that he would visit the same homes maybe two or three times a year.

The basic products he sold were extracts, spices, liniment and ointments. I was quite a big youngster before I knew that these products could be bought at other places as well. I still use Watkins products. They make direct home deliveries the same as they did when my mother was doing the cooking.

Cookware

There were tin dishes which were thin sheet iron or steel coated with tin.

Graniteware was a kind of enameled ironware. It was often blue or gray speckled and chipped easily.

Cast iron was black, heavy and wore well. It lasted forever.

The coffee pot was made of granite. Put in the water, add the coffee loose or tied loosely in a bag, then boil.

Copperware, such as teakettles, would wear well and was pretty but more expensive.

The teapot was an earthenware pot. Green tea leaves were used with boiling water poured over them, and then left to steep.

Earthenware dishes were vessels and ornaments made of baked clay. They were usually quite plain and coarse.

Porcelain table service was of a fine, white translucent earthenware, and was usually very pretty.

Silverware

Sterling silver was lovely, expensive, would bend somewhat easily and would wear indefinitely. Silver plate was less expensive and the silver would wear off after having been used for a period of time. It all needed polishing frequently, even when kept tightly covered. This was a job that had to be done each time before entertaining on special occasions.

Men's Clothing

In the winter, some men had a heavy buffalo-hide or cow-hide coat, long heavy fleece-lined cotton or wool underwear, wool socks, felts and rubbers, flannel shirts, wool pants under their overalls and rubber boots in wet weather.

The following are things men usually wore or carried with them to be in style.

Suspenders — supporting bands over the shoulders that fastened to the trousers and were used in place of a belt.

Armbands — sort of a round garter worn around the arm above the elbow to hold the shirt sleeve at the proper length.

Black buttoned shoes — these had many small buttons up the side and required a button hook to fasten them. I have one of these that was used by my family.

Spats or gaiters — these were fashionable coverings for the ankle and instep which went as high as mid-calf or knee and fastened under the shoe.

Celluloid — a removable collar or cuffs for a man's shirt that was very stiff and resembled ivory in texture and color. They were buttoned onto white shirts and removed when the shirts were laundered. A bow tie was often worn with them.

Derby hat — a stiff felt hat having a dome-shaped crown that was very sharp looking and usually black.

Panama straw hat — a fine hand-plaited hat made in South and Central America from the young leaves of a palm-like tree. These were lovely and expensive hats to be worn in the summer.

Handkerchief — made of nice white linen and worn in the pocket of a suit jacket.

Bandana — a large cotton handkerchief usually red or blue was a necessity for everyday use. It was used for all kinds of things like tying around the neck to keep chaff from going down your back, or wrapping around hurts, even to tie around things to hold them in place.

Gold watch — kept in the vest pocket with a chain that stretched across to a buttonhole in the vest. Very showy.

Jackknife — a large and strong knife used for everything imaginable and carried in the pants pocket.

Penknife — a small and dainty knife, very handy and necessary for "dress up."

Boys' Clothing

The boys wore knickerbockers, a kind of short breeches gathered at the knee. Most of these were made of corduroy, which squeaked when they walked. This was especially noticeable in a quiet place. Corduroy is a durable cotton material with a piled surface of velvet-like ridges.

The blouse or shirt might have a flat wide collar. The tie might be a wide ribbon bow.

Boys dressed in long black cotton stockings held up with round elastic garters. In winter, they put on long leggings (spatterdash-gaiters), extending to the knee, to keep their legs warm and dry.

In cold weather, they wore long, knit stocking caps, or a wool cap with earlappers that had a forepart or a bill.

Boys were not supposed to wear long pants until they were "old enough," probably thirteen or fourteen, and quite big boys. Oh! How they disliked that wait!

Whiskers

Boys thought they were quite grown-up when they were old enough to shave. At this time, there were very few beards, and those were found mostly on the very elderly men. Some men did wear a mustache. Men shaved with a straight razor after covering the face with lather (a foam made with soap and water) with a fine brush. Unless there was a special reason, they didn't shave every day, consequently they would look a little "bushy!"

The razor was honed and stropped frequently, as it had to be kept in perfect condition.

I think when they could afford it, men enjoyed having the barber shave them. He probably didn't nick (cut) them as often as they did themselves! A barber shop shave cost but ten cents.

Ladies' and Girls' Clothing

All ladies and girls had long hair. We weren't supposed to shampoo it very often as it might remove too much oil, so we brushed and brushed it, which was supposed to spread the oil through the hair and give it a natural gloss.

Girls wore long braids, sometimes hanging down their backs or wrapped around the head. Sometimes mothers would wet the hair, and wind it up in rags to sleep on, and in the morning there would be nice long curls that would be pretty for a few days. There were always pretty ribbons tied in our hair.

The ladies always wore their hair high on their heads. They ratted it (we now call it backcomb). Sometimes the combings were kept and made into forms which were pinned to the head wherever they wanted it puffed. The hair was combed nicely over the rats and held in place with hairpins and combs. These were very pretty adornments.

Small curls around the head would be made with a curling iron that was heated in the chimney of a kerosene lamp.

Bonnets and Hats

No female stepped into the sunshine and wind without being protected by a large straw hat or a sunbonnet. No one was beautiful, if tanned. These large brims protected the neck as well as the face.

If one wore short sleeves, the hands and arms were protected with mitts, which were made of worn-out black cotton stocking legs. There was a hole for the thumb to hold the mitt in place and it was pinned to the sleeve with a safety pin.

Dress-up hats might have had wire frames. These frames would be taken to the millinery shop to be covered with velvet or satin material and ribbons. The very special ones were decorated with ostrich plumes. These were very beautiful and costly and could be used many times. My Aunt Eliza Smith gave me one that she didn't want to use any more. I don't remember how old I was, but I did have it on a hat at one time and I still have it.

Mina Todd operated the milliner's shop in Swartz Creek. She was a very stylish lady and artistic in making beautiful hats. Lola Bloss was her helper.

These hats sat on top of the head and were secured with long and beautiful large-headed hat pins.

Dresses

Calico was the least expensive material and was used mostly for everyday dresses and aprons. There were not many pretty colors. All ladies and girls wore aprons to protect the dress and they were especially handy for carrying things from the garden and eggs from the hen house.

Dresses were long with full skirts; most had long sleeves and high collars. Blue and gray were the most used colors. For dress-up, the dress had to be white, probably muslin with gathers, tucks, ruffles, lace, embroidery and insertions (lace or needle-work sewn in between two pieces of fabric).

Some dressed in dark skirts and white waists. There were wool and silk dresses, too.

Undergarments

A corset was a strong garment worn around the middle with steel stays that hooked in front. It laced in back with strings that could be drawn tight, especially around the waist. To be beauti-ful, one must have a tiny waistline, no matter how much one bulged above and below.

Garters extended from the corset to hold up the long, black cotton stockings which everyone wore.

There was a sleeveless knit vest called an underwaist (no

bra), maybe made of white muslin or a wide ribbon with lace or embroidery with drawstrings at both the top and bottom.

The petticoat was gathered full around the waist onto a band which fastened with a button and buttonhole.

Underpants had the same kind of waistband. The legs extended nearly to the knees.

These garments were made of white muslin. There was plenty of cloth with gathers, tucks, ruffles, embroidery, lace and insertion. Also plenty of starch! In the winter, it was the long cotton fleece-lined knit underwear.

Coats were usually long wool ones. A few ladies had horse-hide coats that were very warm. They lasted well until the hair wore off and the shiny hide showed.

Fascinators (scarves) were worn over the head and over hats, around the neck, over the face to breathe through or whatever. Fur neck pieces and a muff for the hands were very warm and very stylish.

Shoes

Shoes were high, black leather, buttoned or laced and not very high heels. At one time, Cuban heels, shaped like an hour glass, were very stylish. Ladies wanted to have small feet. That meant shoes that were too small, and that pinched the feet.

I remember having a pair of black patent leather slippers which fastened with a strap.

Stylish ladies wore silk gloves, carried a fine linen handkerchief and a fancy lacy parasol when "stepping out."

Hobble Skirts

Even in those days, there were fads in clothing. One I remember was the hobble skirt which was a long skirt that was fitted at the waistline, then bellied out until it became so scant at the bottom that the lady could scarcely hobble along. This style didn't last long.

Mending and Darning

All garments and household items were actually worn-out before being discarded. They were mended and darned and mended and darned. Sometimes patches were put on patches. This was a never-ending job. There was always something in the mending basket to occupy your spare time.

Welfare

There have always been people who have had unfortunate and unexpected things happen to them such as illnesses, accidents, deaths in their family, fire, tornadoes and so on.

Family, friends and neighbors would give much needed help. If public help was needed, the township officers, probably the supervisor, would investigate the need. If found worthy of assistance, help would be given. As soon as convenient, the recipient would pay back to the township the amount that he had received, by doing public work, such as working on the highway or roadside, digging ditches, or cutting wood for the town hall.

No one would accept help unless absolutely necessary. It was humiliating to do so, so most families and close neighbors looked after their own.

Fire

The city of Flint was the only place around our area to have a horse-drawn and man-powered fire department. All other areas used the party line telephone to notify people that there was a fire in the neighborhood. When notified, the central or operator in our telephone exchange would ring six or eight short rings on the lines in the area of the fire. Everyone knew it meant FIRE. They all listened in. Everyone grabbed shovels, forks, pails and whatever was handy and got there as quickly as possible.

If water was available, a bucket brigade was formed. This system was quite effective many times. Lives, livestock, implements and furniture would be saved and especially the surrounding buildings.

Household Duties

A specific duty was assigned to each day of the week, and it took much of the day to accomplish it.

Monday was wash day. Two wash tubs full of water would be set on a wash bench or old chairs with a wringer between them. The clothes would be scrubbed by hand on a wooden frame washboard with metal ridges and then put through the wringer to the rinse tub and then wrung once more before being hung to dry. Some ladies delighted in getting the wash on the clothesline before their neighbors and having it be the whitest. You were supposed to have a big washing as that meant that you were a clean housekeeper.

Tuesday was ironing day. You ironed everything, even underwear. Many things were starched and I mean starched! This had to be done when they were washed and then they had to be dampened along with everything else so the wrinkles would iron out easier.

Wednesday was mending day, also darning and sewing on any buttons.

Thursday was for baking—everything! The baking needed to last pretty much for the whole week. This would include three or more loaves of bread, fried cakes, cookies, a pie or cake; all depending on the size of the family.

Friday was house cleaning day. This meant sweeping with a broom and dust pan, washing lamp and lantern chimneys, removing ashes from the stoves, shaking rugs and scrubbing floors.

On Saturday, extra food was cooked for Sunday. Everybody went to town on Saturday night to do their weekly shopping, and also to socialize.

Baths were pretty much a Saturday night event, with a basin of water, soap, wash cloth and towel, if a warm place could be found that was private. Men and boys enjoyed a wash tub of water in the woodshed or some such place where they could splash and spill.

On Sunday, no extra work was done. There might be church, company for dinner, napping, reading or walking over the farm if that was your livelihood. People did much walking on Sunday.

On Wednesday night and Sunday, young men were allowed to go courting. It might be to Sunday night church, just for a buggy ride or he might go visit his young lady and sit in the parlor or take her for a walk.

Entertainment

LARKIN CLUB—People did enjoy catalogue purchasing. The Larkin Company sold their products in this manner. A lady would act as a representative for the company. She would get as many neighbors, friends and relatives as possible to belong to her "Club." The company specialized in such products as laundry aids, tea and coffee.

Coupons were given on the purchases that you made. These would accumulate until you had enough to get the premium you desired and probably could not afford to go to the store and buy.

The representative would also receive premiums according to the amount of sales she made. It was a profitable business if she worked at it and was a good salesperson.

The products and premiums would come in on the railroad and would be picked up at the depot.

The premiums were very nice. I remember my mother getting a combination oak bookcase and writing desk, an oak coat and hat rack that hung on the wall and an oak sewing cabinet that unfolds into a cutting table and has three drawers. I still have the bookcase and my daughter-in-law Barbara has the other two items.

The ladies would meet at the various homes to do the ordering and accept deliveries.

SOCIALIZING — In the winter, someone would take a fast team, sleigh, lantern and bells, pick up the neighbors up and down the road, and go to someone's home for a party.

It might be potluck, but the "real one" would be an "oyster supper." These were quite popular and somewhat expensive at that time. The supper was usually oyster stew and crackers. A certain person, often a man who was especially good at it, would make the stew.

People made their own entertainment which might be held at the church, lodge hall, school or possibly at a home. Card parties were often held at homes or at lodge or Grange halls.

There was always someone good at being "Master of Ceremonies," people good at putting on a play, recitations, singing, music with fiddles, mouth organs and such.

Box socials were popular with each of the ladies making a fancy box lunch for two. It would be auctioned off and she would share it with the lucky gentleman who bought it. The money would be used to purchase something special for the organization that sponsored the event.

And then there were the dances. The music was always home talent. The dance steps were usually the waltz, the two-step and always square dancing.

Chivaree–Charivari–Callithump

A chivaree is a mock serenade. The name and custom originated in France. It was introduced into the United States and is still prevalent in some sections as an attention bestowed on newly married couples.

Late in the evening, after the newly married couple had retired, friends and neighbors would descend on their place with beating drums, rattling tin pans, whistles, shrieks, yells, the firing of guns, and many other discordant noises to rout out the bride and groom.

Its absence in some sections of the country would be regarded as a social slight, but to some people, it was dreaded and disgusting. Sometimes it did or does get somewhat out of hand.

After the noise had proceeded long enough to serve the purpose, the participants were invited in to partake of refreshments provided for the occasion. If by chance there were no treats, which were usually cigars and candy, the groom would be taken by force to buy some. A party atmosphere prevailed before the crowd disbanded.

Teenage Social Games

At parties, many of the teenage games were kissing games such as: Snap 'n Catch 'Em, Drop the Handkerchief, Sly Wink'em, Post Office, Musical Chairs, Circle Tag and Find the Ring.

These parties sort of faded away as people became more sanitary conscious, thinking kissing everyone at every party was not a good idea. Other kinds of entertainment, like dancing, cards and music became more popular. Later movies and theaters took over as "the" activity for an evening out.

THE HOLLAND FAMILY HOMESTEAD

1916, with silo and a new round-roofed barn both of which were conversation topics at the time. This is the farm where the author lived and grew from 1906 to 1923.

THE LINDEN MILL ABOUT 1905

Farmers found a market for their grain in country towns. This grain elevator with mill was on the Shiawassee River.

MY TEENAGE YEARS
1913–1919

These were more prosperous years. Wages and prices for products and farm crops were much higher, making for a better economy.

There were at least three special happenings at this time that were responsible for many changes. They were central heating, automobiles and World War I.

Central Heating

A furnace was placed in the cellar or if a new house, in the basement. The firepot was larger than the one in the stove, therefore it held more coal and/or wood. This warmed the floors and the heat pipes warmed more rooms. A good fireman and good fuel could keep the house comfortable all night long, which was a real blessing.

Anthracite (hard coal) has been buried beneath great masses of earth for thousands of years and hence has been subjected to great pressure and heat. This forced off a great percentage of matter that was converted into vapors and gases, and left a high percentage of pure carbon for us to use for fuel. Hard coal burns slowly and evenly with a clean blue flame. If fired properly, it would burn indefinitely. Fuel was put in at the top and fed automatically into the firepot as needed.

A hard coal parlor stove was an ornate affair. It had a large door which was made-up of framed mica windows. Mica is any group of mineral silicates that separate into thin layers, and is pliable. These transparent forms are called isinglass. When traveling past a house at night, this made a very pleasing light. It was a delightful courting or sparking light, as I found out later.

My parents had one.

Automobiles

Very few cars had been built and sold before these years. They needed to be improved, and people had to have faith that they were going to be useful and not cost too much. By the end of this era, very few families were without one. Soon a car was one item that, after having had one, no one ever wanted to be without.

There were many makes of cars being manufactured at this time. The most popular one was the Model T Ford. The gearshift was with the foot pedal. All others had a stick gearshift.

In 1914, Henry Ford, Dearborn, Michigan, started a new trend and shocked the country. He raised wages to $5.00 for one eight hour day. He figured if he had a production line and made many cars, somebody should have the money to buy them.

Other companies, businesses, farmers and merchants were furious, thinking they would be unable to compete. Men flocked to Ford's to hire in.

Workers did buy cars, since the price was reasonable. It was a huge success.

World War I

Kaiser Wilhelm, ruler of Germany, was the villain at this time. The European War had been going on for some time. The United States got into it April 6, 1917. This was a war, supposedly to end all wars. The Allies won and Germany was defeated. It ended November 11, 1918. Nearly all the young men in the area went. A few didn't come back but most of them did.

People were very patriotic, rallying to the cause, with rationing, buying bonds, knitting, supporting the Red Cross, flying flags, honoring men in uniform, doing any jobs to help the cause. The Country was united.

War always brings about many changes.

Flying

The Wright Brothers, Orville and Wilbur, introduced the art of flying in 1903. It took many years of experimenting for flying to become popular. During the early teen years, flying was mostly fun and daredeviling, but by and after World War I, it had been improved and was becoming quite useful.

The flying machine became known by many names: airplane, aircraft, airship and aeroplane. They all had open cockpits in the early years.

Motorcycles

My first and only ride on a motorcycle was sitting behind a distant relative, who was a middle-aged man. He and his wife came to our house to visit on a Sunday afternoon. I don't think that he had a car. He just loved that motorcycle. He took me for a ride around the yard. I clung to him so tightly, I nearly tore the shirt off his back. I don't think that I was too thrilled. It was somewhat spooky.

Sewing

When I learned to sew, I used a Singer treadle sewing machine that was my mother's when she was first married.

The first garment I ever made was a blouse. It was white figured, light-weight material. It was leftover, so it was all irregular pieces. I had to piece and piece it, which was difficult for a beginner. I put ruffles on it and it was quite pretty. I enjoyed wearing it, probably because I had made it myself. Maybe the piecing was a good idea, as I soon learned I could always make garments out of almost any size or shape piece of material.

I have always enjoyed the challenge of ripping up an old garment, washing, pressing and figuring out what I can make out of it. I like the nicest material I can find when I make something.

The Circus

The first three-ring circus that I ever saw was in Flint put on by Ringling Brothers. Oliver Dart took a few youngsters in his two-seated horse drawn carriage. People always took the kids to the circus. Of course, the grown-ups didn't care about going — just the kids! Ha! I had never seen anything as big as this with so many performers.

We saw the parade travel down Saginaw Street. In the afternoon, we attended the big tent show. I was overwhelmed at the beauty of those girls dressed in all the glitter, spangles and feathers riding the beautiful horses and elephants. For a long time, I just knew that when I grew up I would probably be riding on an elephant's head in a circus.

Country School

My teachers at the Fletcher School beginning in 1906 were as follows:

First and second grades, Chester Severance
Third and fourth grades, Paul McKeon
Fifth grade, William Myers
Sixth and seventh grades, Percy Curtis
Eighth grade, Anna Allen

I guess boys and girls start liking certain ones, even when quite young. Harold Gillies and I always liked each other and we were the same age. I don't know why he did it, but he skipped a grade and then another. I guess if you were a good student, the teacher would let you. He wanted me to skip, too. My parents would have no part of that, which I think was a very good thing.

In the winter, there would be sleigh rides to neighboring schools. There would be arithmetic matches and spelldowns. The room would be crowded, especially the back seats with the big boys and girls and everybody sitting together.

When I was in the seventh grade, the Beebe School, with George Spillane as teacher, visited the Fletcher School when Percy Curtis was my teacher. That was the day I first got my eye on Walter Mitchell. Of course, the boys and girls from another school are much more charming than the ones in your own school. He must have let me know that he *saw* me as there is not much of a "spark" without someone noticing someone. He was the only one that I saw that day. I didn't see much of him for some time, but his family did move onto the Grand Blanc Road farm in 1915, which was next to my grandparents' (Holland) farm. That was quite convenient; especially as I had become a friend of his sisters, Julia and Alice.

I had taken the eighth grade examination when in the seventh grade. I just barely passed. My parents wanted no part of that—I must take the eighth grade. Then I passed with a very high grade. I was a little older than some of the pupils, which bothered me at the time. It was really a good thing. I think there was and maybe still is more practical knowledge taught in the seventh and eighth grades than in high school.

For our eighth grade graduation, we went to Flint to the Genesee County Courthouse. All of the eighth grade graduates in Genesee County were there. It was quite an honor to have passed this exam. We received our diplomas and had our picture taken on the courthouse steps. I don't remember just what all did take place. I think we must have gone there on the train as not many people had cars. That courthouse burned on March 14, 1923. The girls were still wearing the traditional white dresses and big hair ribbons. Most of the boys were still wearing knee pants (knickers) and long black stockings. It was quite a day and a memorable milestone in our lives.

High School

After leaving Fletcher School, I attended Swartz Creek High School. William Hamilton was the superintendent. The school building is now the Friendship Hall, but when it was a school it was much smaller. It had three rooms and three teachers from the first grade through the tenth grade. While I was there, the school put in their first basketball court which was outdoors. I played on the team. Our uniforms were white middy (midshipman) blouses with sailor collars, dark blue ties, blue bandana kerchiefs around our heads to hold our hair in place, as we all had long hair, and dark blue wool serge bloomers which were very full with lots of material and held in place below the knee with elastic, and our usual long black stockings.

The boys wore their usual school clothes when they played basketball.

Mr. Hamilton knew a young lady from Goodrich who worked at the new YWCA in downtown Flint. When the gym wasn't being used, especially in cold weather, we had the use of

1915 EIGHTH GRADE GRADUATION CLASS FOR GENESEE COUNTY

Taken at the east entrance of the Courthouse which was destroyed by fire on March 14, 1923, during a grand jury investigation.

it, and she tutored us. We played a few county teams and lost most of the games, but it was great fun. I usually played forward.

We did participate in some spring tournaments. I remember one being held at Clio High School. At that time, Clio seemed a long distance away. Train service was not convenient to go there. By this time, a few more people owned automobiles. Ralph Freeman, one of the younger boys and not very big, could scarcely see over the steering wheel, but he could drive his father's car. He took the boys.

My parents, by now, had a car and I could drive and take the girls if Mr. Hamilton would ride with me. That made a big day for us to be able to go so far away. I don't think that we did very well in the tournament, but we had a grand time and felt so independent.

We had to provide our own transportation to high school. I drove an old gray mare named Kit. You had to keep a tight rein on her as she would stumble. I would put her in Mason Shaw's barn which was on the Chambers farm. Esther Delaney drove a bay horse named John when she didn't stay with her sister Mary Raubinger. Addie Blair and Beatrice Perry would ride with us. Sometimes I would rather walk the two and three-fourths miles than bother caring for the horse. We girls did our algebra, geometry and sometimes other lessons at home. On the way to school, we compared answers. The person who had a different answer would work it over. We always worked it over and never just copied someone else's answer. I think Mr. Hamilton was suspicious of something. I don't know if he ever figured out why we all had the same answers. When we had an examination and were not sitting near each other, the results would be about the same.

When it came to graduation, we had a three-act comedy play called "Galligar." I was Mrs. Martha Grindem, the principal's wife. It was held at the Oddfellow Hall, which later burned, but was then located where the Fortino house now stands. The other graduate exercises were held at the Swartz Creek Methodist Church. We girls wore our pretty white dresses.

There were eleven of us who graduated: Cyril Ruby, Ralph Freeman, Walter McCaughna, Pauline Davison, Mildred Seigel, Esther Delaney, Ephriam Bedell, George Blair, Beatrice Perry, Addie Blair, and Edna Holland (that's me).

1917 SWARTZ HIGH SCHOOL TENTH GRADE GRADUATING CLASS

Bottom row left to right: Beatrice (Perry) Syring, Ralph Freeman, Superintendent William Hamilton, George Blair, Addie (Blair) Wykes. Second row: Mildred Siegel, Pauline (Davison) Capp, Esther (Delaney) Hiller, Edna (Holland) Mitchell. Third Row: Ephriam Bedell, Walter McCaughna, Cyril Rubey.

4-H

The four H's stand for Head, Heart, Hands, and Health. The 4-H club originated in Indiana and became a national institution in 1914. Dee Perry was the first leader of a club in our area. There were supposed to be at least five members to form a club. Corn and potatoes were about the first projects that I knew about. When I was about 14 years old, I had my one-eighth acre of corn. It did very well.

Four years later, by the time I went to County Normal, other crops, sewing, gardening and handicrafts had been introduced as projects.

Parcel Post

Parcel post came into use in 1913. Small packages could be mailed at any time. People were ordering merchandise from the catalogue and would have to go to town to the depot to pick up the items.

The first amount that could be sent was four pounds. Later it was increased to eleven pounds. Finally it was raised to fifty pounds for short distances and twenty pounds for long distances.

A Barn Was Built

When my father had a barn built in 1913–1914, the timber was cut from the woods, sawed into the proper pieces and let cure or dry for some time. All buildings were built with the lumber from the woods of the landowner at that time. The round-roofed barn was somewhat new and rare. My father looked into the construction of such a roof very carefully and decided that was what he wanted.

The rafters were made and put into the right-shaped forms while the lumber was "green" and left there for some time to be properly shaped, to make the proper pitch for an attractive and strong roof.

John Lawrence was a very popular and good barn builder at that time. He was hired to build it. I think that this was the first round roof barn he had built. His helpers were Herb Bigelow, Edgar Lawrence and Jim Sharp.

One of my jobs was to use the horses and a chain to bring these rafters, one at a time as they were big and heavy, to the proper location for the builders to use.

Jim Sharp was a smarty; he was mouthy and could be a rude person. He especially liked to tease me. I didn't like it, my dad didn't like it and neither did the other builders. Finally my dad said that I should get back at him. My father told me what to say, and that he would stand back of me and support me. So I mustered up my courage. The next time that Jim said something I didn't like, I let him have it.

"Jim, do you know that you should have your tongue split?"

"No, why?" he said.

I said, "So that you can lick both sides of your a-- at the same time."

I thought the other carpenters would fall off the barn with laughter. Needless to say, he never caused trouble after that and was a good friend. I learned the best way to solve a problem of this type is to "catch one at his own game."

I have thought since, it was good that my father insisted that I solve my own problems. I have pretty much been able to do that all of my life. I don't believe in backing down, giving up, crying or rolling up like a caterpillar when things are not at their best.

I was about fourteen when we had the big barn raising with plenty of food. Many people were building nice new barns and houses at this time and everybody came. My grandmother came up and helped mother cook food; we put boards on sawhorses for a table and we all ate outside. People really enjoyed barn raisings; it was a lot of work, but it was a social time as well. Some people even had a dance at night. We didn't have that.

Electric Delco Systems

There was electricity in the city but none yet out in the country, so from about 1913 to 1936, people who were building nice homes were also installing electric Delco systems. They were primarily used for lights and pumping water and gradually other useful items like electric irons and washing machines became available.

Buzz Saws

The gasoline engine and tractor allowed people to make a buzz pile of wood. Neighbors would change work the same way as they did in threshing. A big pile of wood could be sawed in a few hours. This lightened the back-breaking hand sawing and there were bigger woodpiles. People did enjoy these time-saving devices (energy-saving, too).

New Acquisitions

During the years while I was a teenager, my parents acquired the following:

The new barn, of course, which was built in 1914. We also built a garage and a corn crib.

A Patterson automobile which was purchased on July 2, 1915. Part of the salesman's duty was to teach the buyer to drive. As soon as my dad felt capable, he in turn taught me, which didn't take too long.

We built a silo and then purchased a silo filler and a Titan tractor. As the neighbors began to build silos, the men helped one another to fill them.

We purchased a new milking machine with a gas engine. We

PROUD FARMER

Fred Holland leaving his drive to do a job of filling silo for neighbors John D. Burnham, Near Wood and Homer Allen with his Titan oil pull. The tank which is atop the front wheels contained water to cool this single cylinder engine. Notice the symmetrical straw stack.

had five or six cows to milk each day. The milk was set in a tub of cold water and ice from the ice house and stirred until cool. It was then taken to the road by two people either carrying it or pushing it in a wheelbarrow for the milkman to pick up every day.

We bought a new cook stove that could use wood or coal. Coal cost more because we had to buy it; wood we could cut ourselves. Also coal left black soot all over everything.

A set of Johnson Brothers English porcelain dishes was acquired.

Two oak rocking chairs upholstered in leather as well as an oak library table were added to our home furnishings.

We ordered a phonograph from the Montgomery Ward catalog. A few 78 rpm records came with it so we didn't buy any new ones for quite a while. I remember that many of the popular songs of that day were about cars, especially the Ford and the Oldsmobile and we loved listening to them.

My father hired Mr. Mikan who had a tiling machine to

come and put in tile to drain our farm. With the possible exception of their farm which was near Durand, we had the best drained farm in the area. Our farm was easy to tile as an open ditch runs along the east line and through the far side of the wood lot. There were no other people involved. It was a perfect set-up and there were no water holes on the farm.

A Kodak Brownie camera was added to our belongings which took black and white pictures. Many of the pictures in this book were taken with that camera. It was one of the best cameras there ever was!

Social Life — Dating

My parents' rule to govern my social life was no steady dating until at least seventeen and not too often then.

That was no problem as I wanted no part of steady dating or marriage until many years later.

I did enjoy having the boys ask me out, going here and there, now and then. I guess my friends were very kind and did just that. Maybe boys don't like to be rushed into anything either.

"Young folks, no good, going to heck!" It seems as if older people didn't accept the antics of young people very well. They forgot that they were young once. Maybe that is the reason — they remember too much.

My dad had a big dose of that. I guess he was a good listener. If anyone had problems with their children and told him about it, he swallowed it all and believed it. It was terrible and a person might better be in "hell with his back broke than to have children."

I heard so much of this from so many people, that when I was alone, I worried about it and would cry and wish that I had been born years before "when people were born good." I didn't want to be bad and have people not like me.

As I grew up and looked around, none of my friends were in jail or worthless. All of them seemed to be good citizens, working, establishing homes and raising families.

I said to myself, "To heck with it." I am not going to condemn people younger than me. I have pretty much stuck with that idea. I have always enjoyed younger people and still do. I taught school for five years and had a teenage Sunday School class for over thirty-five years and enjoyed every minute of it. Our children and grandchildren have always brought their friends in and I like it!

"Young men think old men are fools; but old men *know* young men are fools." — Goerge Chapman (1557–1634)

Grange Hall

The Grange Hall was located on Morrish Road, just south of Cook Road. Many farm families in the area belonged to the Grange, a farmer's organization, however my parents did not belong. This was a nice community hall where many social activities were held. At this time, it was needed and used frequently. Local people played for dances held there. Cecil Parks, a neighbor, played there, so he and his sister Cora, who were older than I, sort of got me started "partying." I enjoyed this and I guess my parents didn't object to it. Since I was with the Parks' my parents felt I would be all right.

Horse and Buggy to Cars

My dating years were interesting, as it was during the transition from being walked home, being taken in a horse and buggy, and sometimes in an automobile. It mattered not to me as long as I had a chance to go.

My First Real Date

Harold Gillies asked me to go to Swartz Creek to a "Dog and Pony Tent Show." We were both fifteen years old. These shows came for a few performances to the small towns each summer. I never knew if this was his first real date. It could have been, due to our ages. He drove the horse and buggy.

A Few Special Dates

These few dates you might enjoy reading about.

Lakeside Park, on the south side of Flint, was the only amusement park in the area at that time, so it was "the" place to go. July 4, 1917, Homer Whitney, Cloy Gillies, Harold Gillies and I spent the day at Lakeside Park.

Homer's car radiator got hot and boiled dry, which was quite a common occurrence in those days. He went to a house to get some water but they wouldn't give him any. It was city water and they had to pay for what they used. We were hopping mad, as people were always stopping at our homes in the country for something. I guess he finally found some elsewhere. It was a long remembered day.

The Thread Lake-Lakeside Park was opened in 1917. Among the amusements in this park were a penny arcade, pavillions and a roller coaster one-half mile long, a few other rides, shooting galleries and lots of junk to eat, just like now. The park was closed in the 1930's.

A Crazy Date — But Fun

I don't remember how we got organized, but Earl Ruddy, being older and having a car, offered to take a carload of us to

Durand to a carnival that had come to town for a few days. There were all sorts of games of chance, rides and so on.

There were Thresa Ruddy, Addie Blair Wykes and I. The boys were Floyd Brown, Harvey Cole and Fred Sexton. I don't think that we were even paired off. I think that we just kept mixing up. We must have been about 16 to 17 years of age. I don't think that I was ever on a more crazy or a more fun date. I think that Earl enjoyed it too.

No rough stuff — just silly fun!

Paris Candy Store

The Paris Candy Store was on S. Saginaw Street in downtown Flint. They made all sorts of fancy candies which most of us had never had before.

Their ice cream was very special. The cones, sundaes and sodas were somewhat new to most of us as well as the many flavors and colors. All we had known about was homemade vanilla ice cream.

One could sit at small fancy wire tables with chairs that matched. When in Flint, one must go there before going home, especially after going to a movie.

Schiappacassee's Candy Kitchen

This was a short distance from the Paris Candy Store at 518 S. Saginaw Street. It was started in 1886. This store was family owned and operated. Their candy was of the homemade type. They made many kinds and it was the very best. This store closed in 1954. Their second store had opened in the 1920's at 103 S. Saginaw St. at the bridge and closed in 1971.

One of their specialties was their fresh roasted peanuts from machines which set outside the store. The nuts were hot when you bought them. One couldn't resist the smell of those roasting peanuts for some distance away; it sure called the customers to the store. I visited that store whenever I had a chance, as long as it was in business.

Paul "Bo-Nan"

Paul Fortino, was successful and well-liked. He came to Swartz Creek from Italy as a single young man. He started a small fruit store selling bananas (thus the nickname "Bo-nan") and other fruit in the west part of the Fred and Nellie Fuller store building. Later, he added an ice cream parlor. He married, bought property and had a meat and grocery store. Later he enlarged the store and it is still a thriving business operated and owned by his son, Robert and family.

Long Lake Outing

About a year before the horsecar, which traveled between the south Long Lake boat landing and downtown Fenton across from the Fenton House, was discontinued in 1915 due to the coming of more automobiles, Roy, Mary and Floy Burleson, my parents and I had a picnic on the north side of the lake. Then we took the big boat ride across the lake. The boat landing on the south end of the lake connected with the horsecar which took us to downtown Fenton, about two miles away. Several regular trips were made each day.

This was a big outing for me. I didn't know much about Fenton. I had a little money to spend. I was at the age that I just had to have a handbag and I found just the right one. It was a beige-colored, heavy material with heavy lace covering and a drawstring top. It may have cost $1.50, that seems to ring in my mind. I'm sure it was one of my first purchases with my own money.

Livery Stable

The Fenton Livery Stable was owned and operated by the Eddys, located on N. LeRoy Street, opposite the Fenton House. The ten-cent horse barn was used for inside stabling for horses. They also had fine horses and carriages for hire. It was a thriving business, especially good for salesmen and visitors arriving in town by train. The horses were well cared for, they were fed bran mash once a week and were never worked more than six days per week.

Horsecar

The elder Eddy bought an abandoned narrow gauge car line in Muskegon, bringing the rails and car to Fenton. Local citizens helped prepare the roadbed.

This car was drawn by a horse. The car did not turn around. The driver unhitched the horse and put it on the other end of the car. There was a driver's platform on either end. The horse trotted along between the rails. The car was about twelve feet long, with seats along each side for about fifteen to twenty people. Regular trips were made each day.

The big boats, livery stable and horsecar did a thriving business for many years, until the automobile changed people's way of living.

Lake Orion

Lake Orion was a popular resort. We would take the inter-urban from Flint to Lake Orion. One of the main attractions was the big double-decked pleasure boat. We enjoyed the rides around the lake. I think that we took picnic lunches as there were not many places to eat except dinners at the hotels. That was out for most of us. Some of us who went were Irene and Zillah Keener, Proctor Coates, Alice and Belle Heermann, Delia Tibbits and I. I cannot recall the names of some of the others who might have been along with us.

Automobile

July 2, 1915, my father bought a Patterson Car. Part of the salesman's duty was to teach the buyer to drive. I sat in the back seat, watched and listened while my father learned.

When he felt capable, he taught me to drive. My mother didn't care much about it, although I think that she could have driven home if it had been an emergency.

I liked to drive and still do. Beginning at this time, there has always been a car available for me to drive which I have appreci-ated.

Until this date, June 21, 1984, I have a perfect driving record. I have never been "pulled over" or even had a parking ticket. I hope I don't go out now and "blow it." I have driven all over the United States and Canada.

I remember the first time that I took the car alone. My father sent me on an errand to Roy Burleson's which was about one-half mile away. I drove in second gear all the way as I was somewhat nervous and I thought that if anything went awry, I might be able to handle it with less speed.

I must have driven about six years before it was necessary to have a driver's license.

THE FAMOUS LONG LAKE HORSECAR 1891–1915.

Owned by Captain G. Marion Eddy as used to fetch customers for his excursion steamboat from the Fenton Depot for a cruise on the lake.

Recollections of the Prairie Farm

This farm of about three to four thousand acres was located not far southwest of Saginaw, Michigan. It was flat lowland that was ditched with small open ditches, evenly spaced, on this black muck land and owned by a sugar company which raised sugar beets. It was worked mostly with horses and hand laborers. The wagons and tools had very wide steel-rimmed wheels.

I remember the water boy drove a donkey hitched to a two-wheeled cart, carrying a wooden keg of water. This keg had a faucet and some tin cups hanging on it. It was a "welcome wagon" to the field workers on very hot days.

The Prairie Farm raised bountiful crops. The farm was a beautiful place with well-kept buildings and well-bred livestock. It was a talked about showpiece which everyone enjoyed visiting.

One nice summer day, neighbors Barto and Nina Cole, Roy and Mary Burleson and daughter Floy, my parents and I took a picnic lunch and visited there.

THE ESSENTIAL WATER BOY

With his equipment on the Prairie Farm located on the flood plain of the Saginaw River.

Lansing

Another time these same people, plus Dr. and Mrs. Clark (he was a local veterinarian), his son Howard and daughter Gladys and her boyfriend, took the train to Lansing. I don't think that any of us had ever been there before. We visited the Capitol, Michigan Agricultural College and many other places of interest by streetcar.

Genesee County Normal 1917–18

I graduated from the 10th grade at Swartz Creek High School. I don't remember that anything had been said about me having more schooling.

Along in August, William Hamilton came to see my parents and me about my attending Genesee County Normal School. He was a good friend of Genesee County School Commissioner John L. Riegle who had most of the say about the Normal School. For the school to operate successfully, there should be a certain number of people enrolled. The first choices were 11th and 12th grade graduates and people who had taught a year or so after having passed the teacher's examination, followed by 10th grade graduates with good grades and who would be at least 18 years old by the beginning of their teaching year. I would have to enter school a week late to be sure that the class wasn't filled with the more advanced people. I began making preparations just in case I was admitted, which was almost a sure thing as there hadn't been that many applications.

Ella Stevenson, a new friend who had attended high school in Gaines, and I were admitted and I guess that we did about as well as some of the others.

It was a very good "growing up year" for me, even if I had never taught school. It was my first time away from home, although I came back home often.

Most of the girls came from the rural areas around the county. The training was especially designed to prepare teachers for one-room rural schools since most schools in the county were of that type.

I roomed and boarded with my aunt and her family, Mae (my father's sister) and Jacob Berdan and their two children, Claude and Florence, who were about nine and seven years old. They lived on 5th Avenue at the corner of Stevenson Street in Flint and I walked about ten blocks to school.

The teachers were Ellen Anderson, principal, and Rose Walsh, critic, who supervised our practice teaching. We were fortunate to be taught by such capable instructors. The students assigned to Rose Walsh's classroom were those we practiced on. It might have been difficult for the students but it was good training for us "to be teachers!"

The Normal School was located in a few rooms of the Rankin School, an elementary school which was located on 2nd Avenue at Lyons Street in Flint. This school was named after Francis Hamiltion Rankin, a native of Dublin, Ireland, who had settled in Flint. He was a very prominent man. Some of his activities were newspaper publisher, school board member, mayor, post-

NORMAL SCHOOL STUDENTS FROM MICHIGAN COUNTIES

Attending a special field day at Michigan State College in the spring of 1918 before an entrance of Agriculture Hall.

master and state senator. Rankin, Michigan, was first called Mundy Center but was later changed to Rankin in his honor. Then in 1837, when Mundy Township was formed, it was named after Edward S. Mundy who was at that time Michigan's Lt. Governor.

1918 — Storm of the Century

On January 11, 1918, we had one of the most crippling snowstorms of the century. I spent the weekend with Uncle Charles and Aunt Lib Myers who lived in Grand Blanc Township. Their daughter Dorothy (Dot) went to the Normal also. Aunt Lib met us at the interurban stop with the horse and cutter between five and six o'clock p.m. It was a lovely and comfortable ride to their home with huge snowflakes falling. Around ten o'clock that night, the weather suddenly changed. It became terribly cold and windy with blowing snow piling into great drifts all over the place. Uncle Charles had a nice new house with a wood-burning steam-heated furnace which couldn't keep the place warm. He kept "firing." Aunt Lib hung blankets and quilts everywhere. We huddled into small quarters near the cook stove and were still very uncomfortable. The storm lasted pretty much the whole week-end. Everyone was snowbound. The telephones were about the only thing operating. People were stranded everywhere.

As soon as we received word that the interurban was operating again, which was late afternoon on Tuesday, Morris Myers, a son, hitched his horses to the sleighs and took me to the flag stop along with other stranded people. Finally, we got back into Flint. A few local trains were running so I got back to Swartz Creek and home before the night was over.

The storm had covered a large area. Wood and coal were the only source of fuel. Everything came into Flint by train, and they couldn't get through for some time.

To conserve fuel, food and other supplies, all public buildings and unnecessary business places were closed. Priority was given to homes, hospitals, etc.

Schools were closed for three weeks. During that time, people survived and amused themselves as best they could. One evening, a few of us got to Blairs, somehow. We sledded over fences and small outbuildings out into the field. It had been so cold and the wind had blown so hard that the snow was packed, so we just sort of "flew over the top." This was a beautiful, bright, crisp moonlight evening. Oh! What fun!

Cars in Winter

Many families didn't own automobiles. Some of the County Normal girls drove a horse and buggy and put it in the ten-cent shed and walked a few blocks to school. Some of them stayed at the Y.W.C.A. on East 1st Street and worked for their room and board. Some of us boarded with friends or relatives and a few lived in Flint.

People who had cars couldn't drive them in the winter. The roads were not improved and there was no snow removal equipment. Also the radiator would freeze, so they were put into the barn or a shed, drained, covered with a canvas and jacked up so their weight wouldn't damage the tires. When the spring weather came along, the automobiles were brought out of hibernation.

Extra Activity Training

Our class could use the Y.W.C.A. gym at certain times which was part of our training for rainy day games.

In the spring, we took the train to East Lansing to visit what was then the Michigan Agriculture College for some extra teacher training as we taught agriculture and nature study at that time. All students in County Normal classes in Michigan were required to attend this session. They were mostly women who would be one-room school teachers.

We were taught to be 4-H leaders and to have these clubs in our school. Much of the emphasis in our training was on how to manage a large group of children of different ages. It was necessary. You had to know your neighborhood as you were on your own and had to solve your own problems. The school was the center of the neighborhood activities.

My 18th Birthday

For some time as my 18th birthday was approaching, I was becoming more and more anxious about it. I was running in high gear, thinking about making my own decisions, going places, doing things without restrictions and being free as a lark. I don't think that my life had been unduly restricted, or that my life changed too much. I guess just thinking about it and feeling "grown up" was a thrill. I did enjoy it so much that I would have liked to have just stayed at this brink of full responsibility.

By March 8, 1918, it arrived with a "Big Surprise Party," put on by my parents with the help of some of my friends. I usually came home from school on Friday night on the train to Swartz Creek. My parents would pick me up. That helped in planning the party. When we arrived home that evening, the house was full of my friends who came out shouting "Happy Birthday." It was pulled off in grand style, as I was "flabbergasted." It was a nice party. I don't happen to remember any of the party presents.

My Grandfather and Grandmother Holland gave me a very pretty gold watch. I wore it with a fob tucked in my skirtband or pinned to my waist (blouse) with a pretty pin. It served me well. It is still one of my cherished possessions. I can wear it on a chain, which I do sometimes. It runs nicely and is as beautiful as ever.

That evening, as I was on the porch attending to the "good-byes" having had a good time, "be seeing you soon," "thanks for coming," "thanks for the presents," etc., there was one person who seemed to be still just hanging around — just to be last; it was

WALTER MITCHELL AS A TEENAGER

Walter Mitchell. I had seen him a few times as we were growing up since that first time I saw him when the Beebe School visited the Fletcher School. Before he left that evening, he said that I had said to him, "Come up sometime." I guess we were both waiting for some lead, as he was soon taking me back to school some Sunday evenings. It still wasn't too steady. Our romance was somewhat like Topsy, — "It just grew."

I graduated from Genesee County Normal in June 1918. Our graduation exercise was a "flop." For some reason, it was decided that the 16 of us would graduate with Flint Central High School at St. Paul's Episcopal Church. It was not organized. They did not know who we were or what to do with us. We didn't know what to do or where to go. We were just plain "angry." By the time we had graduated, we each had been assigned a school to teach. I signed a contract to teach at the Kline School located on the northeast corner of Sharp and Reid Roads.

Those who graduated from the Genesee County Normal were:

Olive Ackerson	Leila Lymburn
Florence Barrett	Mary Maginn
Edna Holland	Mildred Matson
Flossie Hunt	Florence Monroe
Matie Judson	Laila Ries
Flossie Kelch	Ruth Sevener
Ruth Latimer	Ella Stevenson
Loretta Locher	Lydia Wilde

Our class was a friendly group. We kept in contact and had get-togethers during the years. We lost a few members by death during the 1930's. They were Matie Judson, Lydia Wilde, Ruth Sevener and Ruth Latimer. A few of us have kept together until now. There are only three of us who see each other—Flossie Kelch Hendricks, Laila Ries Rohloff and me. There are four others living—Olive Ackerson, Mildred Matson, Mary Maginn and Ella Stevenson. We have lost track of Florence Barrett.

Kline School September 1918–1920

On the way to school that first morning, I nearly lost my nerve. I thought, "This is a big responsibility. Am I capable of handling it?" Here was a room full of youngsters depending on me. I knew that I could not turn back. That day went very well but I was exhausted when I arrived home. I think that my mother expected such and handled it very well. This feeling gradually diminished, and I soon felt in charge and that I was handling the situation as I had been trained to do.

An odd thing happened late one afternoon at the Kline School during the seventh grade spelling class. Laverne (Christler) Chrysler fainted away and fell from a standing position to flat on his face. He was the largest boy in school and outweighed me by perhaps thirty-five pounds.

Not knowing about "First Aid" and other methods for handling afflicted people, I, quicker than a wink, lifted him off the floor and laid him on the recitation seat. He soon came to.

The unusual part of the ordeal was how I was able to lift him at all, because ordinarily I could not of budged him.

I had been hired for $65.00 per month, which was a very good wage at the time. I suppose that was due to the prosperity caused by World War I. The school board members at this time were Eugene Allen, Dee Burnham and Sanborn Williams.

For transportation to school I drove a pony named Ginger hitched to a cart. Frank O'Brien had bought her for his son Charles who wasn't very big at the time. She was too much pony for him to handle. Frank thought maybe if I drove her to school she might tame down so Charles could handle her. She was about all that I could put up with and she did run away with me once. She was a very nice looking pony. I put her in Ralph and Claribel Close's barn near the school during the day.

During the winter months, I roomed and boarded with the Close's and their son Faye who was about three years old when I first went there. I remember Claribel was an excellent cook.

The Kline school community was a very good community in which to work. There were neighborhood sleigh ride parties. When there were school activities, everybody came and helped. One time we had a box social. The ladies and eligible girls brought nicely decorated boxes with a nice lunch for two. The boxes were auctioned off to the highest bidder. The men enjoyed out-bidding one another to share some lady's lunch. I don't remember what this particular money was used for. Usually it was spent for something the school wanted and that the school board thought wasn't necessary or couldn't afford.

We would have Halloween, Christmas and Valentine parties. We put on our own program, made valentines and drew names. On the last day of school we had a picnic, usually on the school grounds.

My first paycheck was exciting. I remember buying a new outfit. Everything was gray; hat, coat, shoes, gloves and material

MY KLINE SCHOOL STUDENTS, 1919

Bottom row left to right: Helen Pobocik, Lena Kostal, Mary Oleosack, Sylvia Young, John Wood, Pauline Pobocik, Wayne Keyworth.
Second row: Frank Sejak, Mary Nemecek, Marie Burnham, Nora Young, Lyle Short.
Third row: Rose Kostal, Joseph Schlits, Elsie Burnham, Regina Pobocik, Donna Wood, Zelma Burnham.
Top row: Clare Allen, Marguerite Burnham, Josephine Sejak, Laverne Barlow, Clarence Allen.
Absent were Zaida and Laverne Chrysler, Blanch Allen and Silas Coquigne.

for a dress, which was wool worsted, with satin and silk fringe for trim. I intended to make it myself, but I was invited to the Esther Allen-Clarence Derby wedding, and was limited for time so I had Fern Cole, a friend, make it for me.

1918–19 Influenza Epidemic

This epidemic was serious along with WWI. Many people died. It was very contagious. People were required to wear face masks when being out in public. Nearly all social events were cancelled. When in school, everyone gets whatever disease comes along, so, of course, I got it. I have never been so weak before or since. The Swartz Creek doctors, Houston and Clark, had gone to war. There was a Dr. Reynolds who came to Swartz Creek to fill in for them. He was a large, uncouth man, who handed out medicine in big doses, bottles and pills. He was called a "Horse Doctor." The people he doctored who had the "Flu" recovered if they did as he said. Those who did not follow his instructions died. It was a very sad and serious time for our community. There were very few able-bodied people about to care for the sick or to bury the dead.

Fletcher School 1920–21

I stayed at home and walked the mile and a quarter to teach at this school that I had attended as a child. We had 4-H Clubs at this time. All of the clubs in Genesee County held a parade and marched down Saginaw Street in Flint on a Saturday in the spring of '21.

Schools still visited each other for arithmetic and spelling matches as well as baseball games. George Dart and Clifford Vincent were very good ball players. They were recently out of school but came back to play ball with the boys. They were fair with whichever team they played on and their participation made for a very good game.

MY FLETCHER SCHOOL STUDENTS, 1921

Bottom row left to right: R. Ruddy, Donald Steele, Dale Alexander, Lawcock boy, Guy Slocum, Rolland Gilbert. Second row: Two Lawcock girls, Thelma Blair, Gladys Sexton, Nina Steele, Wilma Cole, Ella Parks, Alice Blair. Top row: Richard Gilbert, Arthur Heermann, Otis Bookham, Ward Parks, Dwight Vincent, David Slocum, Ardis Vincent, Beatrice Lake, Eldon Ruddy and teacher Edna Holland.

Grand Blanc Consolidated School

I had a cousin on the Grand Blanc school board and I was interested in meeting new people, making new friends and gaining experience so I hired out to this newfangled consolidated district.

The old Grand Blanc High School had burned and it was being rebuilt so I taught a class in Whigville until January when the new school opened. I boarded with Edward and Mary Schmier at Whigville and Etta and Louise Penny at Grand Blanc. I taught the third grade.

I think that I was better and more comfortable in a country school so the following year I went back to the Kline School.

We developed our own hot lunch program. Our stove had a circulating jacket with a rim about four inches wide and was flat, so we could set something like small playhouse dishes on it for a while before the lunch hour. As the food warmed, it smelled good and tasted delicious. It didn't cost the government or the school district anything.

I always had about 30 pupils. I don't think that I had favorites as I enjoyed each youngster as an individual. I never had any big problems, just a little mischief that could be handled without help and I enjoyed it. I don't think I ever had to physically punish a child.

It would be impossible to remember everyone and the things they said or did, but I will mention a few.

Marie Burnham was especially good at speed tests of number combinations on the blackboard.

Laverne Barlow made posters using vision pictures from poems. A scene from Longfellow's "The Village Blacksmith" was good.

Francis Sejak: In the morning, one of the large boys would build the fire. Then Francis would climb on the top shelf of the dinner pail cupboard where it would be warm first, as the room would be very cold, especially at the floor level.

Arthur Heermann was very good at drawing, making posters, 4-H items, etc. The biggest problem was to get him at it.

Richard Gilbert was being very wasteful with his tablet

paper. I was trying to teach him to be more careful. I said, "It is too expensive to waste. Your father cannot afford to buy so many tablets." He replied, "Oh! He has piles!"

Donna Wood liked to sing and entertain us on party days.

Mary Nemecek would sing for us in Czech.

David Slocum and Laverne Barlow, if given a topic to report on, would come up with a very interesting oral report.

Virgil Young's family rented the Johnson-Truchan farmhouse at the Reid-Linden Road corner when he was about 11 years old. He had shaking palsy and was nicknamed "Shivers." One day he took a washbasin to the flowing well and brought it back about half-full of water. The basin was shaking and the water was sloshing. He said, "Now Shivers-don't spill it." Over it went—all over the floor. He laughed along with the rest of us. We admired him very much. He was a very good-natured lad and did not allow this handicap to ruin his life. After they moved away, I often wondered about the kind of life he had. I admire a person who can "overcome" difficulty and live a good useful life. I know it isn't easy.

Mary Olesak was a very dainty little girl with blonde curly hair. When first starting school, she was so bashful and shy that she couldn't talk to us. Finally, she would smile and whisper. Next, she would come close to me and I would put my arm around her, and she became a talkative little girl.

OUR GROUP AT BYRAM LAKE, 1920

Left to right: Margie White Mitchell, the author, Pearl Morse Hungerford, Lillian Coquigne, Julia Mitchell Gudith all in the latest and most fashionable bathing garb.

THE TWENTIES

This chapter sort of carries over from the teenage years as I am still teaching and doing fun things, such as renting a cottage at Byram Lake and camping for a week during the summer. We did this for 3 years. These are the girls who camped:

Julia Mitchell   Alice Mitchell
Margie White   Pearl Morse
Charlotte Covert   Florence Switz
Lillian Coquigne   Edna Holland

It was a crazy fun thing. I guess the part we girls liked best was getting primped up late in the day — to be looking our best when the boys came in the evening.

Niagara Falls

I think this was the first time on a trip for any of us, at least on our own. There were four of us: Florence Switz, Alice Mitch-

119

ell, Mary Swingle and me. We took the interurban to Detroit, boarded the ship across Lake Erie to Buffalo, New York, then went by limousine to tour Niagara Falls for the day. We were on the ship each night. During the first night, there was a storm and the boat rocked. I awoke in the morning to see the sunrise on the water through the porthole. It was a sight to behold!

We splurged and had a dinner in the state dining room with all the trimmings. The waiters were dressed in black with white shirts, tails and ties. It was the first time any of us had experienced "finger bowls," but we did know about them, which helped.

Summer School, Kalamazoo 1920

Flossie Kelch Hendricks, who was teaching at a neighboring school, and I took a six week summer course at Western Michigan State Teachers College. It was the first time for me to be "really" away from home and also the longest to this day that I was ever away.

This college was small when compared to the colleges of today. It sat on top of the hill. It was 110 steps up to the front of the main buildings. There was a cable car for students to ride. At class time, it would be crowded with people hanging on in all directions.

We traveled by train and street car. For amusement, we would ride to the end of the street car line, get off, look around, then ride back on another car. These cars went all over the city.

One Saturday we took the train to South Haven on Lake Michigan.

Another Saturday, Sells-Floto Circus came to town. We went to see them unload and get set up. This was something we had never seen before. A tent circus was very self-sufficient, doing all their own work, such as: horse shoeing, laundry, sewing, repairing, food, lodging, etc. It was a real business place. A seeing education. "Oh, no," we were not going to the circus. But when it

CABLE CARS AT KALAMAZOO, 1920

The easy way to make the 110 steps to class.

was circus time, we couldn't resist. I guess we had become a part of it. It turned out to be a very nice "all day."

At that time, Kalamazoo was recognized as the celery growing center of the world. We were there.

If my memory serves me well, my subjects were: Nature Study, Literature, Music and Swimming.

It was a very good learning experience.

Ypsilanti, 1921

Addie Blair Wykes, a teacher at a neighboring school, Flossie Kelch Hendricks and a friend and I took a summer course at Eastern Michigan State Teachers College. Being so close to the University of Michigan in Ann Arbor made it seem like just one large community in which everyone was striving to secure more knowledge. I came home at least once during the six weeks.

DEBARKING AT PUT-IN-BAY

All primed for a big day — but where are the boys?

We roomed next door to a noisy religious group whose carryings-on were very strange to us. It was a new experience.

One big event during that summer was an excursion trip to Put-in-Bay. We took the interurban to Detroit, then the boat down the Detroit River and into Lake Erie to Put-in-Bay. We visited Perry's Monument and the beautiful caves. This was my first time in a cave and I was fascinated.

Safety Razors

Safety razors came into being about this time. It was a very welcome device which made for fewer whiskers and nicks and made shaving a more pleasant task, so there were fewer bushy-faced men. Men began shaving every day and became very attractive. I think this was very pleasing to all the ladies and particularly to me.

MERLE G. PERRY, SR.

While on military leave during World War I attired in the standard government issue khaki uniform.

Radio

Merle Perry, a young neighbor, was an inventive type person, always experimenting with something new. After being in the service during the war he had been working on a radio run with batteries. None of us knew much about them.

One Sunday morning he called. He wanted me to come to his

house to listen to his radio. We listened with earphones. He was very happy and excited about his accomplishment and had a right to be.

Cecil Parks

Cecil Parks, our neighbor, would tell me that he knew when Walter came to see me. Mitchells had bought a Dort car in addition to the Model T Ford which they had had for some time. Walter liked to drive the Dort especially well. Like all boys, he would "goose" it. Cars made more noise in those days and Cecil would near him coming. As he approached the bridge (near Cecil's house), he would slow down and come the rest of the way very quietly.

Special Dates

Young people didn't have very many special or expensive dates. I will mention two that I thought were quite special with Walter. We spent one July 4th at Lakeside Park in Flint. That was a popular place to spend the day at that time.

Another time George Mitchell, Margie White, Walter Mitchell and I drove to Pontiac, took the interurban from there to Detroit, then took the boat to Belle Isle. That was a pretty place to visit. It was a very special day.

Joe Pakney

While at the Kline School the second time, a young couple, the Dominic Pakneys, bought the David Bedell farm across from the schoolhouse. As everyone was neighborly and knew the people in the neighborhood, I called on them when their first baby was born. It was a boy and they named him Joe. After all these years, in the 1970's, Joe started farming some of our land and still was up until 1983.

Model T Ford

In the fall of 1922, I bought my first car. It cost $485.00, and I had the money to pay cash for it. Tom Penny was the salesman at Yerkey's in Grand Blanc who sold it to me. It was a touring car with a self-starter, electric lights and electric horn, which made it very modern.

1923 MODEL T FORD

If at that time the 1923 models came out in the fall of 1922, like they have done in the years since then, this picture is really like the one that I had. Ford didn't change the style often. This picture was in The Flint Journal *in 1982.*

Not many girls had a car at this time. I was sort of on "Cloud 9." It was a good car; I took good care of it and it lasted a long time.

In April 1923, my parents rented the farm on Grand Blanc Road at Morrish Road to William Graves. We moved to Swartz Creek into the Miller House, which my parents had bought from the Miller Estate in 1920 and had previously rented out. I lived there about six months until I was married.

Engagement

I received my engagement ring from Walter Mitchell in May 1923. The first thing that I put together for my hope chest was a ball of string or cord. It was a very necessary item and since all packages and sacks were tied with a string it was easy to save and reuse. In fact, I still always have a ball of cord.

I made all of my wedding garments. In August, Walter and I went to Owosso, and he bought his outfit. He left it at my house. We were sort of sneaky and kept our plans a secret, except from our parents. Everyone was asking "if and when." We just smiled and let them wonder.

Marriage

Not many people had big weddings at that time.

At 2:00 p.m., September 26, 1923, at the Holly Methodist Parsonage, the Rev. E.H. Wilcox, who had been the pastor of the Swartz Creek Methodist Church, performed our marriage ceremony in the presence of his wife and the undertaker's wife who lived next door.

After the ceremony, we visited Alice Mitchell, my new sister-in-law, who was teaching school near Holly. I guess we threw her for the rest of the day as she didn't know we were getting married.

To announce this special event, Walter had bought cigars and candy which was the custom at this time. Floyd Larobardiere passed them out in Swartz Creek and Raymond Smith passed them out in Rankin after two o'clock, the day of our marriage.

Honeymoon

We had a wonderful four and one-half day honeymoon trip with beautiful weather. We went to Lansing, Grand Rapids, Holland, St. Joseph, Benton Harbor, South Bend, Indiana, across the countryside to the Toledo, Ohio area, then home through Ann Arbor.

In St. Joseph, there was a religious cult called "House of David" with a leader called "King Benjamin." They had a famous baseball team which played all around the country. Their heavy beards were their trademark, in fact, all of the men in the cult wore beards. The people who joined this outfit gave King Ben all of their worldly goods. They lived and worked and shared everything in this commune. It was a rich, lavish, extravagant place containing many, many acres and buildings.

The public had become suspicious of his organization and were investigating it at that time. It became a newspaper scandal. As we were in the area, we were curious to see the place. They gladly took us on a tour for which they charged a fee. They wanted us to spend the night there, but with all of the unfavorable information that was out, we graciously explained that we should hurry on. We didn't feel comfortable there. We spent the night in Benton Harbor. King Ben disappeared. I don't think that he was ever found. The organization was broken up.

A Day in Flint

In October, Walter's cousin, Russell Penny, died. He was a young man with two small children who had died suddenly, and we attended his funeral in Flint.

We had time that day to have wedding pictures taken, buy a Beacon Blanket and a set of dishes. It was a full set of dishes, which was a service for twelve. They were Grindley Bros. English Porcelain, very pretty, and they served us well for many years. This was our first purchase.

My parents gave us a Singer Sewing Machine and an eight day striking clock. I still have them both and they are still working.

I had taught school for five years by that time. I had my one-year-old Model T Ford, $2,000.00 in the bank and a man. I felt quite successful.

Beryl Brown Hulett

When Walter and I were married, Harvey, Marietta and Beryl Brown lived on the farm next to Mitchells. Beryl was about five years old. Neighbors traded work at threshing time. I guess Walter had talked to her and maybe made a fuss over her. He was her "beau" and she knew that she would marry him. When she would see him in the field or going past their house, she would say, "There's my Walt." When she heard that we were married, she was furious. She was especially angry at me. We didn't know about it for years, until she told us about it and thought it a big joke.

Women's Right to Vote

The twenties had become the "Roaring Twenties."

The Nineteenth Amendment to the Constitution was ratified in 1920. It had taken many years for the men to vote favorably for this amendment. It had caused quite an uproar. Women, like children, should be seen (but not too much) and not heard. Also, I don't suppose they were thought to be intelligent enough to make decisions.

Driver's License

Until about this time, we didn't know anything about a driver's license. We just drove. Now there were more cars, some main roads had been graded and graveled, there was some snow removal as well as more winter driving and more driving problems, so a driver's license was required. This was just something "extra" for those of us who had been driving for some years.

Lindbergh

"Lone Eagle" flew his "Spirit of St. Louis" non-stop to Paris, France, in 1927. Everyone tried to prevent him from making this trip. "It just couldn't be done." He had no financing or encouragement but he and his little plane did it. He had paved the way for long distance and ocean flying and was then given a heroes welcome in Europe and at home.

Prohibition

Prohibition was in effect from 1919 through 1933 and was then repealed. I don't know if it wasn't effective or if the topers couldn't stand it. There had been many illegal "blind pigs" and "home brewers." Before prohibition went into effect in 1919, there were saloons and hard-core drinkers; the average man didn't go in very often and women not at all. After the repeal, the places were "beer garden" and "lounge," often with entertainment. Everyone went in and it made no difference who saw you. It was the thing to do, but you were supposed to be at least 21 years of age.

Public Health

People became very public health minded at this time. Louis Pasteur, a Frenchman, had devised a process called pasteurization which had to do with bringing a fluid to a degree of temperature that was close to the boiling point for a certain length of time so that objectionable organisms were destroyed. This process was successful, especially with milk. Along with this, many sanitary methods were now being used. In the large cities where quantities of milk products were consumed there was less disease. Malnutrition had been a problem among many people, especially children. Milk had been found to be a near perfect food. Now it was not a luxury, but a necessity in a person's diet. Other milk products were promoted and the sales pitch was on.

While prohibition was in force, milk was a profitable business. It was country small talk that after the repeal, the milk business waned somewhat.

Movies

Silent movies came into being about 1900. The words were flashed onto the screen for the viewer to read quite rapidly to grasp the meaning of the story.

In 1928, "talkies" came into being. This was a big improvement. Now, most small towns had a theater which made it possible for nearly everyone to enjoy a movie.

Changes

Times were quite prosperous, and there were many changes. Gone were the celluloid shirt collars and cuffs, ladies' tight corsets and waist lines. Ladies' loose belt lines were around the hips and skirts were very short. There were some colored silk stockings, elbow length silk gloves and store-bought hats that pulled down over the ears. Ladies had their hair bobbed and neatly waved (marcelled). There was a torturous permanent-wave machine that could be moved about on casters. This covered the wound-up curlers which stood on end. This turned on, would produce heat for several minutes which would make the curls stay in place. It was sort of unpleasant, but we endured it. Anything to be in style.

Winter 1923–24

We lived mostly with Walter's parents. He worked at the Dort Automobile Factory. Young farm men would work in the factory during the winter and come back to the farm in the summer. They would always get a job as they were known to be good workers. I did some substitute teaching. For a few weeks, we lived with John and Lizzie Penny. Walter did chores because John had had an operation and was recovering.

Loren McGarvin, a young man from Oklahoma, happened along in the early winter. He was hired to help with the chores and other winter farm work. He was good with horses and taught Charles O'Brien, who was a teenager at the time, some riding tricks.

There was lots of snow that winter, so there were sleigh rides and neighborhood parties. Ed Waterous was sort of a one-man band and provided most of the music for dancing. We played cards and enjoyed lots of good food. These parties were enjoyed so much that they continued for some years.

Mitchell Bros.–1924

In April, Tom and Walter became farming partners and the Mitchell Bros. farming operation was set up. (A year or two later George joined them. Up until that time, he had been working in the factory.)

Tom and Edessa had been married December 26, 1923. Another house was needed. Elmer Gundry was moving to Pontiac to work with his brother in the oil business. He wanted Mitchells to work his farm and Walter and I to live there. That solved our housing problem.

To set up housekeeping, we needed furniture. Tom and Edessa and Walter and I went to Robbin's Furniture Store in Owosso. It was very unusual that all of us liked the same thing since the store was filled with many types of furniture. So our bedroom and dining room sets were alike. In addition, we bought a single day bed that would make into a double bed, two cane rockers, a center table and three 9′ × 12′ rugs. Gundrys had left their cook stove and had a one-register floor furnace in the house.

Other things that we bought, some at the second hand store were: metal bed, three-burner kerosene oil stove with set-on oven, drop leaf kitchen table and chairs, bench ringer, two galvanized wash tubs and a copper boiler; also a washboard.

The Mitchell's were selling cream. Elmer Gundry (whose farm Walter and I moved to) was selling milk, which we continued to do.

We had to cool the milk by stirring it by hand with a long handled ladle before the milk hauler came each morning. The milk can was set in a container of cold water. A windmill pumped the water. Walter couldn't climb. George, who lived where I now live, would climb up and oil the windmill, while Walter in turn would keep George's gasoline engine running to pump his water.

The Gundry well needed repairing. Dorr Russell, the best well man around, did the job. We gave him his dinner. We always served meals to people who helped and anyone else who happened to be around. At one time or another, Dorr dug wells on all of our farms and all around the area, and always repaired them when necessary.

Pet Pigs

Mitchells always raised pigs. One time a sow died and left five newborn pigs. The men brought them to our barn so I fed them from a spoon and soon had them eating and drinking from a trough. We had good luck with them. When they were big enough, the men put them back with the other pigs. Pigs make very nice pets and I really missed them.

Chickens

People were beginning to buy and raise incubated baby chicks. Walter built a brooder house. At first, we heated it with a hard coal burner. Later, we had an oil burner. We had a small fire once with the oil burner, which smothered some of the chickens.

Threshers

For the first few years of marriage, Margie (George's wife), Edessa and I served our threshing meals at the home of our mother-in-law, Agnes Mitchell. There were big gangs of men and boys to be fed when threshing grain from the field. Our men would not let the machine leave for the next farm without all those who worked being fed if it should be near mealtime. One time they really rushed us; they were ready for dinner and it was only the middle of the forenoon. We really couldn't get the big kettles of potatoes cooked enough. They were pretty hard in the center.

Joe Hempstead, who operated the engine (steam), called them "frozen potatoes" and never let us forget it.

Ferns

Rose Morse raised beautiful ferns. I had admired them so much when visiting there when Pearl and Floyd Hungerford and Walter and I were courting, that she said, "When you get married, I will give you one." She gave me a beauty. My parents bought me a nice fernery. I had good luck with it. I started new plants, gave some away and had nice ones myself. After about thirty years, I lost them all.

Sparrows

During these years, sparrows were so numerous that they became a menace. The local governments had put a bounty on them at two cents per head. These were taken to the township clerk, counted (for honesty) and in turn paid for by the township treasurer. These sparrows would roost and nest in the tops of barns and all of the outbuildings and especially in the straw stacks which were in most barnyards. At night while they were roosting was the time to catch them. Lanterns were used to find them. This was a way for young men and boys to earn some extra cash. This bounty business lasted for maybe ten years. It was found to be expensive and not very successful. There seemed to be more sparrows than ever.

Differences

We had been keeping house a short time and eating a meal, (I think breakfast) when Walter sort of sat back in his chair, looked at me and said, "Well, I know one thing. I won't have to worry about you getting mad at me and not talking for a week or so." He didn't want any part of that and neither did I, and it never happened. I liked the way we handled our differences. I don't think we really planned it. It must have just occurred. When we were not getting anywhere with a solution to a problem we changed the subject. If necessary, we would bring it up at another time or skip it entirely. We didn't hurt each other by telling others. We didn't belittle or embarrass each other. He was a very kind and understanding man to live with. I think that we had a very happy and interesting life. I know that I did. If he wasn't happy, he sure hung a darn good bluff.

1925 — A Trip North

Northern Michigan was not very prosperous in those days. Many years later it all changed when tourists and sporting activities brought fame and fortune to the area.

The Maidments, who were Mitchell cousins, from Sault Ste. Marie, Michigan, came to visit the Mitchells quite often. Their son, Russell, was not a very rugged chap. When he was about fifteen, his parents thought it might be good for him to spend the summer on the farm. When school was out, they brought him here and we were supposed to take him home for the beginning of school. The latter part of August, William and Agnes Mitchell, Russell, Walter and I took off for about eleven days for the north. We visited the Mitchell-Penny relatives along the way. It was a good experience for me and I think for Walter, too. I don't think he knew any more about these relatives than I did and when you visit people in their own homes, you learn about the family and their connection.

Our first visit was with John and Belle MacDermaid at Lincoln, Michigan. Their oldest daughter, Maude, was married to Charles Severance and lived in Onaway, Michigan. He worked at a little steering wheel factory. They were expecting, which happened to be the last of their several children.

Not long before, they had lost their oldest son who was about ten years old. He had taken the family cow to be staked to pasture. She became frightened and he became tangled in the rope and was dragged to his death.

We were supposed to arrive at their place in the middle of the afternoon, stay a short while and be on our way because there would be too many of us for them to accommodate. Well! No way could we have left in that manner. Charles was the most hospitable person that I have ever known. He had every reason there was to send us on our way. We were five strangers to him. They didn't have too much room. They had a big garden and lots of delicious sweet corn, plenty of homemade butter and bread as well as some other things. Walter and I stayed at the hotel; every small town had at least one. Charles showed us around the area and we stayed well into the next day. Needless to say, we had a very fine time.

It was a great lesson for Walter and I. They had been so gracious, fed us, put us up, and treated us so nicely.

I said, "If Charles and Maude Severance can be like that— we can be likewise." People have often "just run in on us" and we have welcomed them and enjoyed their company.

We crossed by ferryboat at the Straits of Mackinac to St. Ignace and St. Mary's River into Sault Ste. Marie, Canada. We visited in the Soo, Bruce Mines and Thessalon. We had many

CASTLE ROCK, 1925

Note the unimproved roadway which is now Interstate 75.

relatives living in these areas that we became acquainted with and Russell was home for the beginning of the school term.

It seems that people visited quite frequently in those days, even when they lived some distance apart.

A SOLID OBSTRUCTION

In the middle of Mackinaw Trail, 1925. Taken near St. Ignace, this boulder stood five feet high and was eighteen feet wide.

Cooking Stove

George (Walter's brother who by this time had become a partner in the Mitchell Bros. farming venture) and his wife Margie, and Walter and I thought we needed new kitchen ranges. At that time, very pretty enamel and chrome trimmed stoves were the "in" thing. We looked at various kinds. "Home Comfort" was a very good make. A salesman with a miniature stove traveled about the countryside demonstrating the Home Comfort line. We made an appointment for him to meet with us at George and Margie's. Their son Charles was maybe a year and a half old and sitting in his high chair. The salesman banged, hammered and did some noisy things to prove that nothing could damage his stove. He frightened Charles so badly that it was difficult to calm him down!

Merritt Johnson was operating a hardware store in Linden, which is now called Singer's Ironmonger. He handled Monarch Stoves. He had a dainty green enamel stove with lots of chrome trim. It was a beauty and we purchased it. If we each took a stove, so he could deliver them with his truck and make one trip, he would reduce the price. I think they were $150.00 each. He took off about $30.00 on each stove and we were very happy with them.

Chrysler 1928

We had been driving the Ford Model T open touring car. By this time, the closed (glassed in sedan) was *the* thing and much more comfortable. We bought a 1928 Chrysler, two door sedan. I remember that it was gray and cost about $900 — paid in cash. Everything was paid in cash in those days otherwise people would say, "Well look at that — and they haven't the money to pay for it."

If you borrowed money, it would be for something that would make money for you like a farm, to construct a building, or animals. Frivolities you paid for yourself.

Erma's Birth — February 20, 1929

Erma was born about 4:30 a.m. in Durand Hospital. She wasn't very big and had lots of black hair. Walter and Dr. Covert left the hospital and I supposed they went home. It was 20 degrees below zero, a record breaker, and their cars wouldn't start. They spent the time in the fire department until they could get help in the morning. About 9:30 a.m., Walter came back to the hospital. I couldn't imagine why, until he explained the situation. He spent that day spreading the "Good News." That day Devillo and Etta Perry celebrated their Golden Wedding Anniversary, which Walter attended. They claimed Erma as their "Anniversary Baby." They gave her an antique glass cup with Lincoln's picture on it. It was dated. This cup has always been very special to her. Etta Perry lived to be well into her nineties.

At that time, new mothers stayed in bed ten days or two weeks and took it easy for three or four weeks. Not many babies were born in a hospital at this time. My parents frowned on the idea. The cost in those days was about $40 to $50 and that included about eleven days in the hospital and the doctor's fee.

Dr. Covert from Gaines and a few doctors in Durand had worked hard to get a hospital in Durand. This area was a great distance from other hospitals. They had acquired a two-story brick house, which could care for about eleven patients. There was a head nurse and a nurse second in charge and a cook — that was the personnel. They took turns working around the clock.

Most of the time, Erma and I were the only patients and were "special guests." When we left the hospital, we went to stay with Grandpa and Grandma Holland for about two weeks. They were in favor of the hospital from then on.

Baby Carriage

When Erma was about two months old, we needed or wanted a baby carriage. Alice Mitchell, my sister-in-law, and I went to Sears Roebuck to make the purchase. Alice carried Erma who always resembled Alice in many ways. Everyone was stopping to admire and make a big ado over *her* baby. I was just tagging along! I purchased the buggy which also served as a bed. We placed it beside our bed at night. It was a nice arrangement.

This two-door Chrysler was now the nicest car to carry the baby carriage. The front seat on the passenger side would tip up. The carriage would fit nicely into this space. When Erma was big enough to sit up, she would grab the strap that kept her from falling out. She was at the right height to see what was going on and took it all in.

We never had any difficulty getting her ready to go. Her coat and bonnet were prized possessions.

When it was Saginaw Fair time, Erma was about six months old. We took Erma, baby carriage and Grandma Holland and spent the day at the fair. We had a nice day and I think she enjoyed all of the attention she received, with her big blue eyes and black hair, everyone stopped to pay attention to her.

Fifth Generation

Erma happened to be a fifth generation baby. Aunt Julia Somers Griggs, who lived west of Flint on Calkins Road, wanted her picture taken holding Erma. They came to our house and we took the picture. Julia was the aunt of Libby Myers Heermann, the great aunt of Eva McTaggart Holland, the great, great aunt of Edna Holland Mitchell (me), and the great, great, great aunt of Erma Mitchell Parks.

Edgerton Benson

Edgerton Benson, a Mitchell cousin, would visit the family for a few days occasionally, from Canada. He enjoyed pranks. When Erma was possibly a little over a year old, sitting in her high chair, he gave her a Hershey candy bar. She liked it, was very happy, laughing, flapping her hands with chocolate in her hair, all over her face, her arms, her clothes and the high chair. They were having a high old time. I was horrified, but it was funny!

This oak high chair, with a tray that swung around and a plain round spindle back, had been used by my mother, by me and both Erma and Lloyd who comes on stage in the following chapter.

Overshoes

Erma was small and lively. When she was big enough to do a good job of walking, we bought her a pair of Ball Band one buckle overshoes, the smallest ones they ever made. We bought them at Emery Smith's General Store which was a short distance from Grandpa and Grandma's house in Swartz Creek. She wore the overshoes and walked back to their house, "stepping high." She liked wearing them. We had them bronzed for her instead of her first shoes. They were black rubber with a water-proof black fabric top.

Playpen — Potty-Chair

Walter made a playpen; a frame on hinges that would fold up and store easily.

One beautiful day I decided to put the playpen outside, near the house where I could see it. I put Erma in it and went into the house. She was scared and she cried and cried. That ended that. She did not mind being in it when in the house and we were in sight. It worked nicely on the "opened out" day bed. She couldn't fall and it was warmer than the floor.

Walter also made the potty-chair; these two things were used by both children.

Hands Full

When Erma was old enough to talk, walk and know what we were going to do, especially if we were going somewhere, she would be getting ready, by getting coat, bonnet, mittens, over-shoes, little red chair, rag doll and a little pink pot which was carried in a pretty pink carrier that looked like a tiny suitcase. She would say "hands full — hands full."

She must have been born with traveling shoes. All of her life she would rather travel than do anything else.

About this time, we were exposed to the chicken pox by Cecil and Celia Mitchell who were about seven or eight years old. I was the one who caught them. I was miserable and had a heck of a time. Of course, Erma caught them from me. She didn't take very kindly to them either.

Scovel Farm

In 1929, not long before the "Great Depression," Mitchell Bros. bought the Scovel Farm. It was a mortgage sale and cost $5,300.00. On the north side of Cook Road there were 40 acres, a house, barn, pig pen, and hen house adjacent to the William Mitchell Farm. On the south side of the road was 60 acres, a woodlot, barn and a very good well with a windmill. Douglas Morey lives there now.

November 1929 — Depression

This depression made history. It was considered to be a record breaker for all times. There had been prosperity. Perhaps too much prosperity is what causes a depression. The banks all over the country closed at night, without warning. There was no money available. People who depended on their bank accounts had nothing. Everything stopped. People panicked. There were some people who committed suicide by jumping from roof tops, windows and bridges.

Farmers got along better than most others. Nearly all of them burned wood. Five gallons of kerosene lasted a long time in lamps, lanterns and perhaps an oil-burning cook stove. They raised most of their food, including meat, poultry, etc. They didn't have money but could eat and keep warm. They fared better than the people who lived in the city. Well-to-do people suffered the most. They were in the habit of having all of the things that they wanted and most of us in the country were used to going without. People began to barter. Relatives and friends from the city came to the farms and worked. Food and talents were shared. This lasted quite a few years before the economy seemed to correct itself. It was a trying ordeal.

SOUTH SAGINAW ST., FROM THE DRESDEN, FLINT, MICH.

Flint was our large-market town for most everything from butter to horse hay. This 1909 photo looks north on the main drag during a period of subdued activity.

THE THIRTIES

Our Second Special Event

Lloyd Donald Mitchell was born in Durand Hospital on October 6, 1930. Erma stayed with Grandpa and Grandma Holland for a while. Etta Penny, Walt's maiden aunt, stayed with us for a few weeks until we were back into the routine. She fed us her sugar cookies filled with ground raisins. This was one of her cooking specialties. We enjoyed her stay. I think that she would have made a very good nurse, if she had had training.

Lloyd was a little larger baby than Erma and grew faster. He had some hair, which was a light color. He never could wear the little overshoes. When he could walk, his feet were too big. For a while after he could walk, I dressed them in brother and sister suits. Some people wondered if they were "The Mitchell Twins" who were twins belonging to George and Margie Mitchell.

On occasion, Smith Bridgman's would have an ad in the Flint Journal to have a small child's picture taken free, if you made at least a $5.00 purchase in the children's department. Lloyd was the right age, so he and I went. The children's department was on the fifth floor with a tiny room to change into your

CHILDREN LLOYD AND ERMA

A pre-school photo taken during depression days.

fresh finery that had a high window. Like any small child, he wanted to be held up so he could see and and then wanted to climb right on out. His antics frightened me. We did get one of the nicest pictures of a small child that I have ever seen.

Spring — 1932

We left the Gundry Farm and moved to the Scovel Farm on Cook Road. The farm had been very neglected. During the winter, Mitchell Bros. and Grandpa Holland had been improving the place for us to move into. They moved the west wing from the house to make it into a garage and milk house. The men had removed the varnish from the oak woodwork and refinished it. It was beautiful. They had newly decorated the whole house. It looked very nice and was a pleasant place to live. The well and windmill were on the south side of the road which was very unhandy for household use. We soon dug a good well close to the house, painted the outside of the house and made a nice lawn.

We heated the house with a circulating wood and coal burning stove in the living room, which held a big chunk of wood or a large lump of soft coal.

About that time we acquried two items that made country living within the home much more tolerable — with limitations. They were the gasoline lamp and the flatiron.

The movable lamp was manufactured by at least two companies and perhaps others. The ones we were acquainted with were the Alladin and Coleman. The basis of this invention was the use of a mantle made from a sheath of special thread into which the fumes of gasoline were forced by air pressure contained in a tank that made up the base of the lamp. It was burned within the mantle producing a brilliant white light. This was a tremendous improvement over the yellow flame from a sooty candle or coal-oil lamp.

The gasoline heated flatiron eliminated the necessity of running back and forth to the kitchen range to secure hot sadirons to continue ironing clothes. The heating was done within the portable iron on about the same principle as the lamp, except no fragile mantle was used. A series of regulated small gas torches heated the ironing surface to the needs of the operator. However, these first irons were dangerous as many exploded in women's faces causing some serious injuries.

Harold Peck

When Erma and Lloyd were at the Santa Claus stage, Harold Peck, who lived near by, would come to our house early Christmas morning with a big bag of goodies for them. He would stay until all of the excitement was over.

He was a very good neighbor. We stepped out a few times with them, such as going to a movie. One time we spent the day at the Detroit State Fair. We saw a "Flea Circus," believe it or not. It was fascinating to see those little creatures perform. The man handled them with tweezers and he would get them to do little stunts. I think he called them by name and talked to them. He had little garments on them; they were a little larger flea than what we think of.

Sleeping Temperatures

On hot muggy nights when it was very uncomfortable to sleep, we would take the folding day bed mattress out on the front lawn, just outside the front door. We would be cleaned up and in our night clothes. There was scarcely any traffic. It was so comfortable and beautiful under the stars and sometimes under the moon. About midnight, we would pick up the sleeping youngsters and the mattress, go back into the comfortable house and finish off a good night's rest.

On the other side of the coin, when it was extremely cold and the house was heated with stoves, you would warm one side of your body at a time, then turn around and warm the other side. We often warmed our backs by sitting on the oven door each holding a youngster. The salesman had told us how strong the door was and he was certainly right as it never did show any strain.

Bedtime

This was an interesting time with no rumpus or crying. We would get Erma and Lloyd cleaned up and all ready for bed. We could hold both of them on our laps with our arms resting on the chair arms, hold a book, read, look at pictures or whatever.

Never talk down to or underestimate the comprehension of a child. Erma was old enough to make some reading decisions. We had a child's version of "Uncle Tom's Cabin." That was the one that she wanted. I told her that it might be too difficult for Lloyd to understand. She insisted—I gave in. The next morning Lloyd got up and came up good and loud with, "And Phineas Fletcher drove the horses."

Sometimes we would get sleepy before Erma and Lloyd. They would turn and look at us. This went on until there were too many long arms and legs. Then we sat on the davenport. Everyone would be so sleepy, we would just "tuck them in" and sign off for the day.

Herbert Hoover

Herbert Hoover was president at the time of the Great Depression (1928–1932). Of course, he was hated, abused and accused of causing all things "not good." No one person can cause such a disaster. It builds up over many years by many people.

He lived long enough to again become a hero and a very useful man for his country. This doesn't happen very often.

Franklin D. Rooevelt

Franklin D. Roosevelt became president with pomp and glory, to get us out of the depression — right now. He established some three letter agencies to create temporary jobs which were badly needed, such as WPA. This consisted of cleaning ditches, clearing roadsides, improving highways and other public works. If a work project could be finished in a week, it sometimes would be stretched to a longer period to provide more working time. This encouraged shiftlessness among otherwise good laborers. These projects were supposed to be temporary, but many people took to this type of employment and this system became permanent. This fostered inefficient work habits that have stayed with us to this day.

Rural Electrification

This was the best project that Roosevelt promoted. Before, cities and towns were the only areas that had the use of electricity. People had been flocking to the cities to partake of "the good life." Now this changed.

To secure electricity for use in the countryside, people were required to petition the utility company. There needed to be a given number of "sign ups" and guaranteed users within a required distance to extend the line. I think the electric companies were afraid of losing money on these rural people. They set a minimum monthly rate which was $2.58 per month. Soon people were using much more electricity than the companies anticipated. It was a big help to farmers and they were ready to accept it. The electric companies were surprised that it worked as well as it did.

People now started buying small acreage and building nice country homes and enjoying fresh air and scenic open spaces. It changed country living. There was no reason to move to the city to have the use of modern conveniences.

F.D.R. was the only man ever to be elected to the Presidency of the United States for a fourth term. He died while in office. I remember one of this famous quotes, "The only thing we have to fear is fear itself."

Family Tragedy

February, 1933, George Mitchell died at the age of 37. He had had appendicitis attacks over a period of time. The doctors were skeptical as to his problem and never wanted to operate. The appendix burst, and peritonitis took over. Antibiotics were unknown.

In November of that same year, another tragic event happened that affected our entire family.

While walking home from the Rankin School, the eleven year old twins, Celia and Cecil Mitchell, were the innocent victims of an automobile accident at the southeast corner of Grand Blanc and Linden Roads. Celia lived only a few hours. Cecil's leg was permanently injured. It was a debilitative handicap, but he was plucky and never allowed it to affect his life.

This was especially difficult for their mother Margie, after having lost her husband the preceding February.

1933 Chicago — World's Fair

Money was still not very plentiful. We had never been to Chicago and The World's Fair was being held there. This was a double thrill, which might be a chance of a lifetime.

Alice Mitchell was teaching school. She had a new Model A Ford, which we took. Alice, Ethel Penny, Walter and I went. Grandma and Grandpa Holland took care of Erma and Lloyd.

We stayed outside of the city in a sort of rooming house and had a place for our car. A young man, who was part of the

THE MITCHELL TWINS

A photo taken a short time before the accident which was witnessed by a group of neighbors who were meeting at the Mitchell home nearby.

establishment, would drive us in our car to the fairground each day and pick us up each night. He also drove our car on a tour of Chicago, which included Maxwell Street, the Stockyards, Marshall Field, etc. One evening, we took a waterfront boat ride which gave us a beautiful view of the city. It was a real thrill. We were gone on this trip for about a week.

Long Lake

Long Lake became Lake Fenton. Since there were 106 Long Lakes in Michigan, and due to the location near the Village of Fenton, it was thought for identification that a name change would be an advantage, this lake being very popular with the moneyed people from the big cities.

Dr. Mark Knapp had lived in the area since 1910 and became interested in the idea. He circulated petitions for the change of name to be made. Of course, there was strong opposition to the change to be overcome (some bitter pills).

This lake is about five miles long and one-half mile wide and contains about 850 acres in parts of six sections.

Our Watkins Man

Each salesman had an area that he visited three or four times a year. For a number of years our salesman was an older man, a bachelor, who went from house to house throughout the countryside calling on farmer's wives. If we were not in a big hurry when he came, we enjoyed his visits and would learn something. I remember at least three topics of conversation:

Asparagus: We wondered why people put salt on it. This vegetable originated on islands in the Pacific Ocean and was watered with the salt water waves.

Specked Apples: As a child, his parents had an orchard with lots of apples. The cellar was full of beautiful apples. They always had to eat the ones with the spots first — so by the time they got to the last ones — they had specks, too. They never got to eat a perfect apple!

Muggy Weather: He grew up in Illinois near the Ohio River. That locality was noted for weeks of hot, muggy weather every summer. If he came to our house on such a day and we complained about it, he would immediately halt the thought, as he had vowed not to complain about our Michigan summers and would say that we knew nothing about hot summers. He thoroughly enjoyed our Michigan summers.

An afterthought; one time he came just after we had finished our dinner. The table had not yet been cleared. I had made some soda biscuits and there were a few left over. They were especially good ones, but they were cold. We liked them hot. I noticed that he was eyeing something on the table. Finally he mustered up enough courage to ask if he could buy a couple of those biscuits. I told him that they were cold. I also told him he was welcome to them, but I wouldn't take any money. He liked cold biscuits when he couldn't get the hot ones, or maybe it was the home cooking he liked.

Childhood Illness

Erma and Lloyd had the measles and whooping cough. Erma had scarlet fever. We had no idea where she picked it up, as she had not yet gone to school. At that time, we were quarantined for 40 days, with a red sign on the front of the house. No one was supposed to come or go. Walter lived upstairs. He carried a basket and climbed a ladder. Erma was the only one to have it. Before we were freed, I had to wash and clean everything in the house. I was fortunate to have acquired a washing machine for this task.

Electricity was starting to come into the rural areas. We didn't have it yet, but the people on Torrey Road had recently obtained it. Some people we knew had a Maytag gasoline motor for sale. We bought it and found an old washing machine to fit it. We had to "hunt." We found a sorry looking one at a dealership in Flint for $20. It looked so bad that we covered it with a blanket so no one would see it when we brought it home.

Walter took it all apart. We cleaned, painted and bought new parts. It looked like new and ran like a top. The exhaust was vented out through the window. It had cost us about $45. It served us as well as a new one which would have been $175.

It sure saved the day for me for the quarantine cleanup.

The Children's School

Erma and Lloyd were now attending South Mundy School. Marie Wells was the teacher.

At the center of the community activity were the South Mundy Church and the school which had a very active PTA. We made most of our own entertainment, such as plays, music and suppers and socials.

The children went with us to all of these functions and took part. Everyone took their children wherever they went. We didn't know much about "baby-sitters." If we couldn't take our children, we didn't go.

Erma as a small child decided she would always go to PTA— she enjoyed it so much.

Clubs

While we were living on Grand Blanc Road, the neighborhood ladies had organized a sewing club. It started out as a "Meet and Chatter" and then we started bringing sewing to work on as we talked. We would have a potluck dinner at noon and then spend the rest of the afternoon at the home of the hostess. This continued for many years even after we had moved to Cook Road.

Another group of women formed a Community Card Club. We would play progressive pedro and this one had a potluck lunch, too.

The husbands from these groups would be invited to a few special events during the year. During the summer, there might be a picnic or two at someone's home or at a nearby lake. We might roast hot dogs, marshmallows, have watermelon and homemade ice cream.

Other times it might be a Halloween, New Year's Eve, Surprise, Farewell, or a House Warming Party.

Mitchell's had a big farm truck, with a high stock rack,

canvas and bales of straw. Everyone would climb in and away we would go, singing and laughing all the way. There was always plenty of eats.

PTA

I became Chairman (now Chairperson) of the South Mundy PTA and attended the Genesee County PTA Council. I was secretary of that organization for a time. I had a chance to help on the planning committee for the State Convention, which was held in Flint at the famous Durant Hotel. That was a worthwhile experience.

One time I attended a State Convention at Battle Creek with a carload of ladies from Genesee County.

One of the ladies was a leader. She had had more worldly experiences and took more chances than the rest of us. She knew someone with authority at Jackson State Prison. She called him to make an appointment for a tour of the prison on our way home, which would be in the evening long after visiting hours. She would blink her car lights a certain way to be admitted so we wouldn't be shot at. We had a better tour than the people who went during the regular visiting hours. We were locked behind two sets of heavy iron gates. It gave us a "scary twinge." We were grateful to this lady for a new experience.

Church

I was involved with the South Mundy Church in a similar way. We were called the "Ladies Aid Society." At each monthly meeting, we would serve a dinner. We served neighbors, our men, and the children from South Mundy School. Adults paid 25 cents and the children ten cents for their dinner. We also had our annual chicken dinner and bazaar.

There was no well at the church for many years so we carried the water from the school or our homes in milk cans.

In a country church, it took the women to get things done and keep things going so — "Let the Ladies Aid Society do it" was more than a slogan.

Sunday School

I started teaching a teenage Sunday School class at the South Mundy Church in the mid-thirties. I had the class long enough that the first teenagers had their own teenagers come to my class years later. I enjoyed those young people very much. We took special trips to places of business which were unfamiliar to us and also a boat trip on Lake Erie from Detroit to Cleveland. During the winer months we had parties at various homes. I retired from teaching this class in 1972.

Prince and Fanny

Nearly all farmers had a tractor, but most of the farm work was still done with horses.

Mitchells raised several colts. I will mention my favorite, a very beautiful and graceful dapple gray named Prince. He was a show horse and smart, sort of roguish. He would sometimes get loose. He had a big area in which to roam. With his head held high, his mane and tail flowing in the breeze and high stepping, he would circle the area in the most beautiful manner. We would try to catch him with an ear of corn as bait. He would get just so close, then be off again. You could just sense his tease. After having had his fun, he would come to you as good as could be.

Tom Mitchell had taken the Berry Horse Training Lessons when a young man. He trained colts, then we sold them. I don't

OLD FANNY

Enjoying herself as much as the youngsters who are left to right: Lloyd, Bruce and Erma Mitchell.

know why they sold Prince, probably because he was valuable. Maybe we needed extra money.

A mare named Fanny had served Mitchells well for many years. She now had become quite old and was safe for the children to play with. We had an old harness and a buggy frame with a box on it. Hope, Bruce, Erma, Lloyd, all the cousins, and neighbor children had fun either riding horseback or on the various contraptions behind faithful Fanny.

Peter Pan

After Fanny died, we bought Peter Pan as a play horse for the kids. He was a good-looking small bay horse and was an especially good riding horse as he had been trained for polo playing. We had him for a long while. He finally became sick with lockjaw and we lost him, too.

Buggy Wheels

Lloyd was playing with some buggy wheels that were attached to an axle. He started to ride them down an incline near the house. They turned over, threw him backwards and cut a gash on the back of his head on gravel stones. It was a bad cut and left a lifetime scar.

Even old-fashioned playthings were dangerous.

I Gave Our Pigs to Moreys

I.B. Morey lived a short distance down the road from us. Morey and Mitchells each raised white pigs. We had about 20 nice 150 pound pigs at this time. They got out of the barnyard on Grand Blanc Road, came down the lane, through the woods and up the Scovel farm lane and through our yard. Evidently, they had turned around by our house and headed back when I first saw them. I supposed they had come up the road from Morey's. I called Martha to tell her that their pigs were at our place. None of the menfolks were around so she walked up. She and I drove them down the road to their place. The story goes that you can't drive pigs where they haven't been before. They went without any trouble, turned into their yard and into their barnyard as the gate was open. We shut them in. They seemed like "happy" pigs.

When the men got around later in the day — the joke was on ME. They were our pigs.

1936

This was a very hectic year. We were putting hay into the mow in the barn which was very close to the road. To draw the hay up, we hitched the horses to the rope that pulled the slings full of hay to the top of the barn. This caused the rope to be stretched about three feet high across the road. There was not much traffic and we watched very carefully. This time we were caught. Marion McKeon came buzzing down the road real fast. She didn't see the rope across the road and we couldn't stop her. WHAM!! She held her car very well. There was no harm done to her or her car but Erma was standing near the barn. When the rope snapped, it flew back and hit her. She had a bad rope burn.

Also that year, Walter was bitten by an old sow! He had a shot for lockjaw or whatever just in case.

When the house of William J. Mitchell, Walter's father, burned on June 13, 1936, at what is now 5247 West Grand Blanc Road, most of the contents was saved with the help of neighbors.

The fire was caused by sparks from the chimney igniting dry cedar shingles.

An amusing thing happened within this tragic event. As usual there was a large cast iron range in the kitchen. I remember well when it was placed there. It took four men and it was about all they could do. Two men, Frank O'Brien and Frank Seldon, carried it out when the house was afire, the reservoir was full of water and the hot firepot was full of ashes. It just goes to show the strength of two men under abnormal conditions.

At the time of this house fire, the hospital was calling the family to tell them that the mother, Agnes Mitchell, could be released.

Bertha Mitchell (no relation) was operator at the telephone office in Rankin. She had to deliver this message. A very unusual coincidence.

Agnes was having a very painful bout with glaucoma. One eye was removed thinking that might save the other. It didn't work that way. She lost her sight. When she was released from the hospital, she stayed with her sisters in Grand Blanc for a few weeks. Then she was treated in Ann Arbor Hospital. When leaving there in August, they came to live with us while they were in the process of building a new house. Our household now included William and Agnes Mitchell, a nurse helper, the hired man, Al Kuchan, Erma, Lloyd, Walter and I.

By New Year's, the new house, to replace the one burned in June, was finished. William and Agnes moved into it. They now had electricity, which made for comfortable living. It was necessary for them to have a housekeeper as Agnes was now blind.

I recall two opinions of Agnes while she was living with us. A high-powered lady evangelist came to Flint at this time for about two weeks who was supposedly healing everyone who had an affliction. Many people were attending these meetings and becoming very excited about "the healing." Two neighbors became very overwhelmed and came rushing to our house to persuade Agnes to attend a meeting to regain her sight.

She, in her quiet way, said, "No, I will not go. I don't have that kind of faith." I, too, think it was a big farce.

She was concerned about being blind, getting helpless and living in that condition. I said, "You have a family and many friends."

Agnes replied, "As time goes on, they become few and they forget." With good personal care, she stayed with us for three more years. She was very appreciative of everything that was done for her. She died quite suddenly in August, 1939.

1937

At the time that Mitchells moved into their new house, I was quite sick with pneumonia. I didn't recover as rapidly as it seemed I should. Then Walter went to the Owosso Hospital for a hernia operation. A few weeks later, George and Laura Penny invited us to a Sunday dinner of their own baby beef and home-made ice cream. That did the trick. We both recovered very well.

Most of the farmers welcomed jury duty in the wintertime when they weren't real busy outside. Walter's name was drawn for Genesee County jury duty and he served for six weeks at the Court House in Flint.

Al Kuchan, our hired hand, enjoyed hunting, trapping and fishing. He spent the winter living in a cabin on Bennett Lake south of Linden. He had told us that he would invite us for a muskrat dinner. He had a nice dinner and believe it or not, the muskrat was very tasty.

Electricity

We were now getting electricity on Cook Road. By May, 1937, it was available. First, the buildings had to be wired and the light fixtures put in. Appliance agents were invading our premises like ants. The first thing that I wanted was a washing machine motor. Our gasoline motor was now in bad shape. It leaked oil, had a bad oily smell and the machine vibrated and jumped around the room. This was the same old Maytag that Walter had cobbled up years before and was second-hand to begin with. We paid Sears Roebuck $6.50 for the electric motor and Walter put it on. I had it to use as soon as the electricity was turned on. Was I happy! A few weeks later, we bought a nice flatiron from George Blair and it was a jewel, too.

Vacuum Cleaner

Later in the summer, a Regina vacuum cleaner salesman was sure that Edessa and I needed a vacuum at the tune of $80.00 each. We didn't think that we could afford it, although we liked the appliance.

About six weeks later, he came back with two sweepers priced at $50.00 each, saying that instead of receiving money for his commission he had asked the company if he could have two sweepers. He was sure that he could sell them to us at this price. He did and was happy. He had made money by selling them to us for more than the commissions he had due and we had saved money. They were good sweepers and served us for many years.

Dodge Car

In 1937, we bought a used 1936 Dodge for $600.00. We sold our old two-door Chrysler to a neighbor. This Dodge was a nice car for teen-agers. It was very dependable and we had it until Erma and Lloyd got out of high school.

Axminster Rugs

By this time, we needed new rugs. Our rooms were large, so we bought a 11′ × 15′ and a 15′ × 15′ Axminster rug. They were very pretty and wore very well.

Piano

Thinking that Erma and Lloyd should have an opportunity to take piano lessons, we bought a used Cable piano from Grinnell Bros. for $60.00. It is a very good piano and stays tuned. They took lessons from Mrs. Hinkley of Linden. Erma also took some lessons from Bessie Johnson Delanoy. I had taken lessons as a child. We always liked the music as provided by the children in our home.

Typhoid Fever

One summer three of our neighbors, all at about the same time, had typhoid fever. We all panicked, had water tested, were vaccinated and did everything that we thought would be a preventative. We never knew how or why it came about. Those who had it were:

Kate Riley, who was an elderly lady and was quite ill. She recovered.

Donna Aspin was about 13 or 14. She was seriously ill. For a time it was thought that she might not live but she did recover.

Calvin Beckman was about ten then. He died.

1937 — Strike in Flint

General Motors Auto Workers had tried unsuccessfully to organize a union. A sit-down strike was called. This was almost unheard of at that time. It was a serious and tense situation and lasted for many weeks. Frank Murphy, Governor of Michigan, and Circuit Judge Gadola of Genesee County were the outside help used to keep the strike from becoming dangerous and getting out of hand. The UAW was recognized as the exclusive bargaining agent and became very powerful as a result of this action.

1939

War had been going on in Western Europe for a few years. Hitler was in power in Germany. He had set out to conquer the world. England had now declared war, which would affect Canada. When this news was announced on the radio, Douglas Dodge of Arthur, Ontario, the Edward Passingham (Sarah Gunn) family of Sarnia, Ontario, and Annie Gunn of Toronto, Ontario, happened to be spending the week-end with us. The news really frightened and saddened them.

I informed them that they were related to each other the same as they were related to the Mitchells. Quite a coincidence.

Douglas invited us to visit his home for a few days. He was not yet married. He would take us to the Toronto Exposition, which was a grand affair, and we were anxious to attend. This was a very short time after war had been declared so there was very tight security everywhere, such as soldiers, guns, etc. The atmosphere was tense and scary. We could really sense it while we were in Toronto.

We visited Annie Gunn and her sister, Rachel. Douglas was now very family oriented and wanted to get to know his relatives better. These meetings were really the origin of the Scott Reunion, which started in 1950. Walter's great-grandfather, Alexander Scott, had come from Peebles, Scotland as a printer to Canada. Many of his descendants are living in Ontario and Michigan.

Color Movies

This year was the beginning of color movies. Until this time, pictures had been black and white. Needless to say, they were beautiful and accepted wholeheartedly.

At this same time, two movies were made which became famous and have been shown frequently, even to this day. They are "Wizard of Oz" and "Gone With the Wind."

40th Wedding Anniversary

We had a surprise party at our home honoring my parents, Fred and Eva Holland, on their 40th wedding anniversary.

William and Lilly Wiggins (my father's sister), Thomas and Nina Penny, and Hosea and Alice Young were seated at the table with them as honored guests. These four couples all grew up in the same community, were married during the same year and were lifetime acquaintances.

I wrote the following poem for this occasion.

Two Score Years

By Edna Mitchell

'Twas in those days of long ago
    That Cupid with his darts
Set out with determination
    To pierce those youthful hearts.

So what seems to be
    A world wide way
They would set aside
    That glorious Wedding Day.

So on October twenty-five
    In the year of ninety-nine
It was happily decided that
    I'll be yours if you'll be mine.

It seemed to be
    With determination grim
That she did decide
    To make the best of him.

He with all the ups and downs
    Which do just occur
Made up his mind
    He must put up with her.

Now comes the waiting
    During that expectant whirl
It turned out to be
    Not a boy — but just a girl.

Hardships and catastrophies
    Have been but few
Perhaps just enough
    To hold life more true.

Over such a span of years
    Some changes we would note.
But just a few of them
    Would be wise for us to quote.

It appears those golden tresses
    Seemed to turn to gray
While some of them
    Just vanished — or went astray.

Also there has been added
    Now and then — a pound
But take it all around
    They seem to be quite sound.

So life most interesting has come
    During these years — two score
We wish God most gacious will be
    And grant to them — many more.

A Merry Christmas

Charles L. Wells,

Rural Letter Carrier. **Route No. 1**

A FREE CHRISTMAS CARD FROM THE MAIL CARRIERS

Mr. Wells was one of the early rural carriers from the Swartz Creek Post Office. Note the details of his rig.

THE FORTIES

The Railroad Steam Engine disappears in favor of the Diesel Engine in 1941. I missed the graceful "Iron Horse," the shrill steam whistle on a cold crisp morning, the white high-rising steam and smoke against the clear blue sky and those huge smooth turning wheels.

WORLD WAR II — 1941
A SURPRISE ATTACK

Japan bombed Pearl Harbor on December 7, 1941. This was a shocking event. Many lives were lost and many ships destroyed. War was declared and fighting started immediately. We were also fighting Hitler in Europe. There were many casualties, imprisonments and much destruction. Many items went off the market so the materials could be used for making war equipment. Food items like butter, meat and sugar were rationed.

Finally, Japan surrendered and Hitler was defeated after all

of the cruelties and the suffering he had caused. Supposedly he
ended his own life. This war had lasted about four years.

William Mitchell's Housekeepers

Following Walter's mother's death in 1939, William had
some housekeepers. There were two that we became very friendly
with and helped out by running and doing errands and taking
them places, especially to church and neighborhood affairs.

I remember Verna Burton who was one of the housekeepers
saying, "Edna, it is just awful to be old, JUST AWFUL!" When
she was not able to stay and help any longer, Walter and I moved
her along with her belongings in our farm truck to Houghton
Lake to live with her daughter Beulah who was operating a motel
and restaurant and making delicious pies for it. Verna had her
own apartment and spent her last days there.

Estella Knight was the other; she kept her home in Swartz
Creek so if for any reason she would leave, she would have a place
to live. A niece, upon whom she depended, died, which left her
without someone to look out for her. She put in an application to
the Whaley Home for elderly ladies on East Kearsley Street in
Flint. There was a waiting list. When her turn came, she had to
go or lose her turn. She sold her house and went. The Whaley
Home was a beautiful place. It was formerly a wealthy family's
home which contained their lovely furnishings.

The home put on two birthday parties for the ladies during
the year. The parties were for winter or summer birthdays. Each
lady could invite a guest. Estella invited me once. It was the
grandest party that I have ever attended.

Walter was sort of special to these ladies. If they needed or
wanted something, he was good about seeing that they got it.
Along toward the last, Estella said to me, "Edna, don't you
EVER let him get away from you."

Township Clerk

I was elected Mundy Township clerk for a few years. At that time, a caucus was held to determine the Democratic and Republican candidates to be voted for on Election Day. The officers were: supervisor, treasurer, clerk, justice of the peace and two trustees. The meetings were held in the Township Hall located on the southeast corner of Grand Blanc Road and Jennings Road. The hall was torn down many years ago.

The township was mostly farms. There were very few houses on lots; hence, the population was sparse.

The supervisor handled what welfare there was. It was mostly short term hardship cases. These people were almost ashamed to ask for help. They would be assigned to some township work, such as digging ditches, wood cutting, road work or cutting weeds to pay for the assistance they had received.

Some of the problems the township board had to handle were petitions concerning digging or cleaning of drains, settling line fence squabbles and problems with dogs damaging flocks of sheep. Sometimes a justice of the peace would be called on to decide some of the knotty problems.

Moving — September 1942

We moved back to Grand Blanc Road, where I now live in 1942. We had worked all summer getting the place ready. We set up the dairy here for 20 to 25 Holstein cows. We bought and moved the small building from George Chrysler's to be attached to the barn to be used for a milk house. We piped water from the house to the barn and put in new stanchions, individual water bowls, a DeLaval Milking Machine, a hot water tank, a refrigerated cooling tank and tubs for washing milking equipment which was all done in this building. We also put up a silo. We were in big business with modern equipment.

More Poultry

We bought and raised baby chicks for years. We raised Leghorn pullets and sold eggs. For a few years we raised White Rock broilers. The heat lights were the most satisfactory way to warm the building. We always bought the day-old chicks early in the spring, about 100 at a time. At about five months they began to lay. Broilers were kept about three and one-half to four months until they reached about six pounds.

House

We made quite a complete overall plan for the house and lawn. It was about twelve years before it was the way we wanted it. We stuck with the plan, did first things first and did a few at a time as we could afford it.

The first things that we did before we moved in were to build a new chimney from the ground up, put in a forced-air wood and coal furnace, build a new stairway to the second story, build a dormer window on the east side of the north bedroom, and newly decorate the whole house.

Dentures

At about the same time, I was in need of dentures. It took about three months from extraction to new dentures. Dr. Canfield did the honors. I think he was one of the best denture makers that I ever knew. One of my objections to false teeth is when meeting a person, you see them first. The dentures he made were not noticeable and others remarked that they were comfortable to wear. I told him there were two requirements that I would insist on. I must be able to whistle and eat sweet corn on the cob. He was quite sure that would be possible, and it was. I had some other good help as I was struggling with them. The man who installed our milking machine, Lewis Gale of Davison, had dentures a year or so before and had some good tips. When biting off food such as sweet corn or apples, you press in very firmly until the food is entirely bitten off then remove it. In that way one can eat any food without tripping the dentures and having to resort to a knife or to end up not eating favorite foods.

Erma and Lloyd in High School

Erma had passed the eighth grade from South Mundy and was entering high school at Swartz Creek. Lloyd would be in the eighth grade. During the interim, we had moved from Cook Road to Grand Blanc Road and were now in the Rankin School District. It seemed the best solution for Lloyd to take the eighth grade in Swartz Creek, as he would have transportation, so we had to pay his tuition to Swartz Creek, which was $45.00 for the year. At that time, parents had to provide their children's transportation. As it happened, which was very unusual, there were three sets of brothers and sisters from this area who were attending Swartz Creek High School. They were: Alvin and Dorothy Parsell, Bruce and Hope Mitchell, and Lloyd and Erma Mitchell. Each family was responsible for transportation every third week. It worked very well.

A few years later after Alvin had graduated and was working, he would drop Dorothy off at our place for an hour or more each morning so she could catch the bus for school. By now Swartz Creek had bus transportation for students. I called Dorothy "my other daughter."

Adolescence

At this time our children (I should call them young people now) were active in 4-H Club projects. They both had Holstein calves. In addition, Lloyd was enrolled in handicraft and Erma in sewing. I encouraged their participation, maybe too much sometimes, because I had been acquainted with this activity since its beginning and knew it was good for country kids in many ways. These projects are developmental vehicles that young country people ride to adulthood.

Sold Farm

Soon after we moved to Grand Blanc Road, Mitchell Bros. sold the Scovel Farm on Cook Road to R.C. and Frankie Terryah for $7,200.00

16th Birthdays

Erma had put up quite a fuss about having a birthday party for her sixteenth birthday with both boys and girls invited. We had not acted very interested as far as she could see and she was somewhat disgusted. We really surprised her with a big party and it turned out well.

When Lloyd's sixteenth birthday came along, he wasn't much concerned about a party. We had invited all his cronies in and he didn't realize that it was a special party for a while! He just thought they happened to come at the same time.

Lloyd on His Own

When Lloyd was 16 and in the tenth grade we let him take the car for a few days (that old dependable '36 Dodge). He filled it with his friends, Chet O'Brien, Jim Stevenson, Bob Gould and Ted Smith who was on crutches with his leg in a cast. They took off for up north, and since we, the parents, had said so much about writing home, when they got to Swartz Creek, they stopped and bought cards with scenes of Swartz Creek. They wrote on them telling what a nice pretty place it was, that they liked it there, then mailed them. We just about cracked up.

Being on their own and not knowing just how far their money would go, they spent lavishly at the beginning and soon ran out of cash. At the beginning Lloyd had hidden enough money to buy gasoline to get back home. They ate mostly from people's gardens and were nearly starved when arriving at our place about 7:00 p.m. four days later. They wanted a chicken dinner. I told them that I could get them almost any kind of a dinner, except chicken. That would take too long and be too much work. They *insisted*, so I assigned each one to jobs. They worked like beavers. They killed, picked and cleaned the chickens, peeled potatoes, set the table, etc. About 11:00 p.m., they had their chicken dinner. I guess they had been snacking all the evening, but they sure devoured that two-chicken dinner in a hurry.

The Kids and the Car

By now, we had owned the '36 Dodge for some years. Erma and Lloyd were teenagers and thought it was a little out of style. It was a very dependable car. They were allowed to take it and were careful. Some of their friends, whose parents had new cars, were not allowed to use them. Our car was always filled. They were always allowed to call home if necessary if they needed help.

We never stayed awake or paced the floor while they were

out. It seemed that about the time that they were supposed to come home, I would awaken. They usually talked to us about their adventures of the evening before going to bed.

A few times, Lloyd especially, would try to outsmart us. He used several schemes, such as: coasting into the yard, leaving the door unlatched, taking his shoes off and tip-toeing in. Of course, the stairway was over our bedroom. I didn't admit it to them, but I think both of them slipped in a few times without being heard.

Combine

Combining standing grain in the field dealt a death knell to large threshing crews and spelled the end of neighborhood meals put on by farm women for these crews. Both the men and the women missed these events for opposite reasons. The threshing machine seemed to be on its way out and combines were on the way in. This meant no more barnyard straw stacks. It also led to straw and hay baling in the field. The hay loader, hay car, track, pulleys, ropes and slings were not being used. A conveyor now placed the bales into the barn. It was still hot dusty back-breaking labor.

Lloyd's Pigs

Erma and Lloyd pretty much handled their own money— such as it was, not too much. They were both good financiers.

Lloyd, unbeknown to the men, bought ten or twelve newly-weaned pigs from George Stevenson. Walter and Tom didn't know just how to handle this one. He had to buy his own feed. He bought corn from Arthur Cupit. He had very good luck with them and made money. When he took them to market, he had the farm truck full of nice looking pigs. On the way, he stopped to show them to Stevenson who was surprised and happy that Lloyd had done so well with them.

Graduations

Erma graduated from Swartz Creek High School in 1947. She went to General Motors Institute for two years. Her class was the last class of girls as the course was discontinued. She got a job at the Chevrolet plant on VanSlyke Road in Flint after completing her education.

Michigan State University, at that time, held agricultural short course terms each winter. Erma thought that she would like to enroll; it was possible to take leave from work with General Motors to attend school. She enrolled in the Home Economics course and by the time she had finished, she was offered a job at the college in the Agriculture Extension Department. She explained the situation to Chevrolet and off she went. This was her first time away from home.

Lloyd was a half-year student and graduated in 1949. He took a job at the Buick in Flint as well as helping on the farm.

Shrubbery

When we planned our lawn, driveway and house painting, we had three hurdles to jump. Our house is high, long and narrow. The first project was planting the shrubbery around the house. We contacted Genesee Nursery on Hill Road, which was owned and operated by George Curtis. Aaron Muchler was employed there for many years. We wanted the planting done early in the spring. We contacted Aaron while the snow was yet on the ground and before George Curtis had returned home from Florida. He came with his measuring tape, drawing board, etc. He carefully selected the proper shrubs for each side of the house according to the wind and weather conditions. He was very particular. When George Curtis returned from Florida, Aaron showed him the plans; he approved them without making any changes. This was the first planning Aaron had ever done completely on his own. He was so proud, he "burst his buttons." He cared for it on his own and kept watch over it for years.

Sometime later, I saw Mrs. Curtis. She said, somewhat disgustedly, "I don't know why Aaron makes such a fuss about your lawn."

I said, "I do."

When I told her why, she said very kindly that she would encourage him. We had set a maximum price of $250.00. It did the trick.

1948

We did some special improving on our home. We put in our circle drive and lawn. The work was done by George Chrysler. He knew his road building and had very good equipment and was very particular. He had been a road builder when he was a township highway commissioner. He did much hand work, especially around the maple tree by the road which was very close to the former driveway. It had been there for years and never grew to be much of a tree, but with moving the driveway, and George's tender loving care, that tree took off and as one can see, it is now a large tree and still growing.

Little House, No More

We had the room, now we put in the fixtures, and we had the use of a bathroom. No more outhouse out back.

The "little house" in itself wasn't so bad. It was getting out there when the need arose. At various times during the year there would be strong winds, a pouring rain, an ice storm or even a blizzard. You went at nature's call to the little house all the same. Sometimes with great inconvenience if it happened to be in the middle of the night!

Also, now we had a walk-in shower. No more hunting for a place of privacy where you could climb into the old wash tub for a couple of minutes. You just closed the door.

Convertible

Lloyd wanted a convertible like all the young fellows were buying at that time. It was the "in" thing. We weren't too anxious about it, but he had his own money and was pretty much on his own. He found a pretty red 1947 Plymouth that he could buy for $750.00. His father and Grandpa Holland went with him to look it over. He bought it. Walter and I drove it a few times and took it on a trip once. Everyone thought we were "quite sporty." Lloyd was satisfied and didn't want another one. The moral here is: It may be wise for those youthful and reckless desires to be fulfilled when one is young and not wait until you are middle-aged.

Television

People started buying televisions in the late 1940's. The picture was black and white. It became popular quite fast. When driving around the countryside, people would watch to see who had antennas and would then know who had "splurged" and bought a television. It was enjoyed so much that friends would invite people in to watch it for an evening.

We didn't have one until 1952 when Lloyd returned from the service and purchased one.

Women Drivers

In the earlier automobile days, a few men took possession of their cars and no family member, especially the wife dared touch or drive it. Children were careless and women weren't supposed to know enough. "Oh, those women drivers!"

We knew a couple of men with that kind of thinking. We were discussing this topic one day. Of course, I had been driving ever since I was 15 years old and had bought a car when I was 22. I thought that was a terrible and restricted way to live and was thinking about how I would handle such a situation, when Walter said, "You would just up and leave the S.O.B."

THE FIFTIES

Dick and Janet Weeks

One day a young married couple in a big old car with all of their possessions showed up on our doorstep. It was Dick and Janet Weeks, Mitchell cousins from Washington, D.C. They were on their way to California. Dick had lived there as a small child. They were on their way to visit friends and relatives and possibly to get a job out there. Dick's Aunt Emma McGee told them to stop here on their way. Emma was Walter Mitchell's second cousin. Dick and Janet stayed around for a few days and then took Erma with them to Sault Ste. Marie, Canada to visit some other relatives.

They asked Lloyd to go to California with them. He decided it best and safest to take his Plymouth convertible. They were traveling across the country with a credit card and no money. They had their own camping equipment and were gone three weeks before they had to get back here as their credit card was about to expire. They couldn't go on until Dick could earn some money, so he got a job. By now, it was late summer and time for canning. Janet helped me and we worked it out so she would keep some of the canned goods on shares. She was very proud of her accomplishment.

One day Dick was visiting with me in the kitchen as she was coming down the stairs and overheard him say, "I never knew Janet to work like she is working here."

She said, "I know it, and I just *LOVE* it."

When he had earned enough money, they moved into an apartment in Flint. They invited us to a Sunday dinner that Janet had prepared. It was very good.

Dick had a couple of hobbies. One was that he bought, made and painted parts for a huge electric train. He had done a very nice job on it, and everything worked perfectly. One could scarcely get around the room because it was so large.

He also took flying lessons at Bishop Airport and took Lloyd for a ride. After a few months they became homesick and went back to and settled in Washington, D.C.

Korea

Lloyd was drafted into the army for two years. This was during the Korean War. He went first to Fort Custer in Battle Creek, Michigan. We visited him there. He then had his basic training at Indiantown Gap, Pennsylvania, near Harrisburg. He had just bought a new Chevrolet, which Erma bought from him. He had three black Angus feeder cattle. The men sold them for him when they were ready for market.

Walter, Erma and I visited Lloyd at Indiantown Gap. He had a long week-end pass. We picked him up and went to Washington, D.C., and we visited the Weeks family. Dick's brother Jack drove our car and showed us all of the beautiful sights and places of interest in the area.

Erma flew home to Lansing, and we took Lloyd back to camp. We took a few days coming home, which included a tour of Hershey, Pennsylvania, and hunting for a wooden pepper mill like the one the Weeks' had. We finally found one in Bowling

Green, Ohio. I liked it so well that I have always had one since then.

Mother's Illness

My mother had a stroke while Lloyd was in the service. She recovered quite well. About ever so often, she would have another stroke and recover at a little lower level each time. This covered a period of about four and one-half years. She went into a coma for about a week and died in her own home in June 1956. She had been a very good patient during the time that she was a semi-invalid.

75th Birthdays

During this time, we had a nice surprise 75th birthday party for my father at our home. We had a dinner with twelve people present.

Three years later, on my mother's 75th birthday, we had an open house party at our home. It was like a family reunion.

Lloyd's Return

Lloyd had been in Korea. Near the end of the time to be spent there, he was injured. He was sent to a hospital in Japan. When he was able, he was sent back to Fort Custer. He was discharged in a little less than the two years.

Madge Billsbrough

During the years of my mother's illness, my father had hired Madge Billsbrough, a neighbor about my age, to help care for her. I became acquainted with Madge. We worked very well together. She was very depressed and discouraged at that time. I invited her to bring her washing to our house. We did many kinds of work together. We started making garden at our house. We both enjoyed gardening, and we also did all of our canning, pickling, kraut making, etc. here. This was therapy.

We continued to be friends for about 30 years until her death in 1982.

30th Anniversary

Walter and I had been married 30 years on September 26, 1953. Erma and Lloyd bought plane tickets for my parents and Walter and I to fly from Bishop Airport to Willow Run near Ann Arbor. It was a 27 minute ride. They drove to the airport to pick us up and take us out to dinner.

Flying was a new experience for each of us. Walter did not like heights and did not want to fly. As we were getting ready to go to the airport, Walter cornered me saying, "Now if I can't get on that airplane, I don't want you to go raising HELL!" He got on. It was a beautiful day and a delightful trip. He enjoyed it but was never anxious to go again. He said that if it was necessary he would, but he never did. My parents enjoyed it. Of course, I enjoyed it and have gone on several trips since.

Tornado 1953

One of the worst disasters to strike Genesee County was the Coldwater Road and Beecher School area tornado in June of 1953. There were 650 people injured and 113 people killed. Buildings, trees and everything was demolished or carried away.

1954

William Mitchell, Walter's father, died after a short illness in 1954 at the age of 88. He had still been living in his own house. He had had a successful cataract operation when 80 years old and he had been able to see very well for the remaining years.

Swimming Lessons

After having enjoyed recreation in, on and near water all my life, finally after I was over fifty years old, I took swimming lessons and learned to swim. My buoyancy must have been good because the instructor told me that I could float on my back, read a newspaper and smoke a cigar all at the same time. Of course, I never tried it.

In the deep end of the pool I could stand upright without touching the bottom and with a bit of finger and toe action move about at will. When it comes to fast swimming I am not the best, except in salt water where it seems to me I can move much faster.

Painted House

Our house was badly in need of a paint job. I studied it from every direction very carefully. The way the house is built and with the two kinds of siding and the trim, I could visualize a two color paint job. I wasn't getting much cooperation. Some people can't imagine how things will look before the job is finished. Since I always liked to swing a paint brush I took on the project on my own. I went to Gudith Hardware in Holly, which was owned and operated by Emery Gudith, our brother-in-law. He handled a very good brand of paint. I purchased some white paint and the items that I needed. I painted the window frames first. Emery helped me select the proper shade of green that we thought would make the house "beautiful." We selected Laguna Green.

I started painting the lower areas first and worked my way into higher areas. I was somewhat nervous, so I said to myself, "You old fool, why get scared? You came up here to paint, not to fall, so get those silly notions out of your head." I guess that did the trick. It didn't seem to bother me after that. As I went higher, other people got nervous, so I got help to do the rest of it. People started telling us how nice it looked. I never had any problem keeping the house painted after that.

Modern Kitchen

We also modernized the kitchen in that year. We built in birch cupboards, a counter top, a new sink, put in a fan over the stove, had new windows put in and installed a lazy susan in the cupboard. We finished it all off with a new tile floor. My father did the work for us just as he had done all of our remodeling over the years. At that time, it was a very modern and pretty kitchen.

Kline School Get-Together '54

The girls, now ladies, who had gone to school to me in 1918, had talked and talked about getting together for a party. Nothing happened until my daughter Erma and Bernice Vojdik, Kathryn Sejak Vojdik's daughter, became acquainted in Lansing, where both of them worked. They got Kathryn and I together. We set a date for a party to be held at my home in November, 1954. Many came and we have been meeting each year since. Some of us hadn't seen each other for years. It is a gathering that we each look forward to.

These are the people who have been coming to the parties over the years.

Amanda Burnham Monroe	Pauline Pobocik McGuire
Elsie Burnham Dougherty	Regina Pobocik Harcik
Marie Burnham Roth	Mary Nemecek Vitous
Marguerite Burnham Stubblefield	Stazie Nemecek Hlavacek
Helen Pobocik Klapko	Clara Spillane Barnett
Kathryn Sejak Vojdik	Julia Smith Kiefer
Mary Olesak Gach	Anna Trubiro Skrceny
Henrietta Trubiro Howath	Nora Young Thomas

Sylvia Young Survan (deceased)
Donna Wood Rockwell (deceased)
Anna Kostal Trecka (deceased)
Rose Kostal Shultz (deceased)
Lena Kostal Lazenga (deceased)
Edna Holland Mitchell — I was the teacher.

This list is of May 1983.

Scott Family Reunion

The Scott Reunion really began in 1950. As I have mentioned in 1939, the thoughts had been jelling, people contacted and ideas brought to light. In October, 1950, on the Canadian Thanksgiving Day, we met with Edward and Sarah Passingham, near Sarnia. It was a very, very rainy day. Many people came from far and near. Nearly all were strangers to someone. They are the descendants of Alexander Scott, who had migrated to the Teviodale, Ontario, area in the early 1800's from Peebles, Scotland, having been a printer there. His wife had died in Scotland. Later, he brought his children with him to Canada, where he married a second wife and had another family.

It is unusual that several generations later, the two families are so loyal to each other and this family reunion. About as many relatives live in Michigan as Ontario, as well as a few living in other areas. People look forward to and wouldn't miss this reunion. Now, with so many families having campers, it has become a weekend affair.

It is held the first weekend in August, which is the Canadian Civic Holiday. At this time (1983) with the large attendance and the many campers, we hold the affair at a Canadian park and campground east of Sarnia.

Cattle Congress — Waterloo, Iowa

In the spring of 1954, Morley Hayden (Walt's cousin Bertha's husband) was transferred from Niagara Falls, New York to Rapid Falls, Iowa. When moving, the family, Morley, Bertha, Jack and Judy, stopped at our place for a day or so enroute to Iowa. It was planned that we would visit them in October and take in the National Cattle Congress that was held annually at Waterloo. This was a gala affair. As we were making our plans, Walter came up with the idea of asking Cecil and Annie Campbell of Thessalon, Ontario, to go with us. Walter, Bertha, and Annie were cousins. The Campbells came from Thessalon to St. Ignace to meet us.

We drove west on Route 2 with beautiful Lake Michigan's blue water and white sandy beach on one side and autumn colored forest hillsides on the other gleaming under the bright sunshine. This made for one of my most memorable days. We also visited the Wisconsin Dells and Blue Mount Cave. We came home on a southern route through Peoria, Illinois. We were gone about a week and then the Campbells stayed with us a few days before going home by bus.

Farm Bureau

The men in our family had been active in Farm Bureau since the early 1920's. In the 1950's the Women's Committee was formed and I was the first president in our local neighborhood group. Up until this time farmers had not been able to really afford health insurance. The Farm Bureau gave group rates to members and this allowed many farmers, for the first time, to be eligible for insurance at affordable rates.

As president of our local neighborhood Farm Bureau, I was assigned to attend the Genesee County Farm Bureau Women's Committee meetings and I became secretary of that group. Later, I was Vice-President of our District #5 Group, which is comprised of Eaton, Ingham, Clinton, Shiawassee and Genesee Counties. I enjoyed the work. It is a very education-minded group of farm women.

Farm Bureau sponsored an essay contest in 1958. This was my entry which took second place.

What Freedom Means to Me

Our Creator, when making heaven and earth, gave man dominion over all. Then, few men must not have dominion over others or some will live in fear, humiliation and suffering.

God sent Moses to deliver the Israelites from Egypt. So He has sent leaders all through the ages to free man from dominating forces.

We find in the Declaration of Independence, "We hold these truths to be self-evident, that all men are created equal, that they are endowed by their Creator with certain unalienable Rights, that among these are Life, Liberty and the pursuit of Happiness. That to secure these rights, Governments are instituted among Men, deriving their just powers from the consent of the governed."

Freedom allows man to be himself. No human being has reached the degree of perfection he must reach. Human progress depends not only on God, but on the effort made by each man individually. By giving man conscience and freedom of choice, God gave him this responsibility. Man must have liberty. Without it, he cannot progress. Each individual can mold his own destiny.

Our forefathers, the Pilgrims, settlers of the Colonies and others were seeking religious freedom as well as freedom of state. They were dissatisfied with taxation without representation, so they came to this country. Now, our Constitution guarantees them these freedoms and more, also the right of an individual to own a home, to save, to invest and bequeath to one's children.

Lincoln once said, "You cannot bring about prosperity by discouraging thrift; you cannot strengthen the weak by weakening the strong; you cannot help the little man by tearing down the big man; you cannot help the poor by destroying the rich."

The three departments of our government are very just and fair. The legislative laws are made by many men from all walks of life and all parts of the country, which makes complete representation.

The executive branch carries out the enforcement of these laws, as intended when they are made.

The judicial department keeps men from being falsely

accused and punished. One can testify his case and have a trial by jury, which gives one as fair a chance as is possible in the presence of men.

We build tomorrow's world today. There is power and there are possibilities of people trained to work together effectively. There are no bounds, an individual may think, say or work for what he believes. His acts are voluntary not drafted. Men may make the possibility of truth more important than the possibility of error. He may present truth through his personality. The only horizon to the future will be the limit of Man's imagination. Instead of fear and failure, there will be faith and triumph. The concern will not be private gain but public good. If one fails, he can start again and keep trying.

Look for real values. Man reaches high and noble achievements only as he recognizes his divine obligations and meets them in high hope. If there are no visions, the people perish.

Freedom is not easy. People have to keep working for it. That is what keeps it progressing and why we have enthusiasm. It makes a firm foundation. Like in Matthew, we find, "The wise man who built his house upon the rock; and the rain fell, and the floods came, and the winds blew and beat upon that house, but it did not fall, because it had been founded on the rock."

Opportunity is for all, regardless of race, color or creed. It matters not on which side of the tracks one is born and raised. All have the same chance for prosperity and public service.

Ideas and decisions made by all people by vote, are of more value than rules made by a few self chosen rulers.

Popular opinion is very effective and has much strength. It could not exist where freedom does not prevail.

Man, to do all the good he can in all the ways and times he can, can only accomplish this where freedom exists. He must have the desire for accomplishment.

The trees are free to bud, the sun to shine and the birds to sing, so shall it be for man to live. The long best view to the free man is ahead.

Now, how does this relate to me as an individual?

When my son was in service, I had the privilege of visiting our Nation's Capitol. I gazed at the Capitol and other government buildings, the flag gently blowing, the monuments to some of the important men who helped form this freedom, Arlington Cemetery, where there were the many who had worked and given their lives. I was filled with pride as I thought of this vast country with its national resources and the many people it represented, and that I, with other individuals, was a part of it. I belonged.

I believe, and have faith in our democratic free country. To prove my faith, I have many duties and obligations. To name a few, I should:

> Keep informed so as to know the truth.
> Not make up my mind until I know something about both sides of the issue.
> Accept the facts, whether I am for or against the question.
> Decide what is right—then go ahead and act.
> Dare to do right, even if by doing right I might be different.
> Help select good, honest people for office.
> Never miss the opportunity to vote.
> Accept civic duties, which I am capable of doing.
> Accept the costs to maintain this freedom.
> Forget prejudices in race, color and creed.
> Do unto others as I would have them do unto me.

These ideas and statements on, "What Freedom Means To Me," should be appreciated by all in our land. These are the things that make us happy. Happy people do the most good for mankind.

Like it is inscribed on the Liberty Bell, we will, "Proclaim Liberty through all the Land and to the inhabitants thereof."

Horse and Carriage Barn

This barn had not been kept in good repair. It was badly in need of siding and a foundation. We engaged Mr. Luther Hahn from Flint, who was one of the best building movers in the area to move it to the south onto a cement block foundation. We put on new siding, doors and windows and painted it. It cost about $2,500.00. It looked pretty sharp when the job was finished and is still a very useful barn.

OUR OLD HORSE AND CARRIAGE BARN

On the skids, well on its way to a new foundation and rejuvenation toward becoming our general purpose barn.

Florida

On our trip to Iowa in 1954, we and the Campbells planned a trip to Florida for the future.

In 1957, we took a western route through Indianapolis, Indiana; Nashville, Tennessee; and Birmingham, Alabama. We toured much of Florida and visited relatives and friends. We really enjoyed the citrus fruit and strawberries grown in the Plant City area.

We came home by an eastern route, through eastern Georgia, North and South Carolina, Virginia; we traveled the Pennsylvania Turnpike and on through Ohio. As it was our first visit to the south, it was very educational.

Polio

In the early 1950's, there had been a polio epidemic. This had been a very serious disease causing crippling paralysis. About this time, Dr. Jonas Salk discovered a very successful vaccine. The disease is very seldom heard of since that discovery. It has been a blessing to humanity.

Color TV

People had been enjoying black and white TV for some time. Now color had come on the screen and became popular very rapidly. It wasn't long before people were trading in the old sets for the new beautiful colored sets.

FARM HOME OF AUTHOR

The old carriage barn, as moved and rebuilt by Luther Hahn and his right arm Big Ed, is the middle structure.

Marriage

Our son Lloyd was married to Barbara Mills on December 26, 1956. They lived with us for about two and one-half years while their house was being built by my father, Fred. They built it along as the money came in. It is built on Linden Road on our farm. Cindy, Tammy Sue (who lived about 10 hours) and Lloyd Junior were born during the late 1950's.

1957

Mackinac Bridge, stretching from Mackinaw City to St. Ignace, had been under construction for some time and was opened to traffic in November, 1957. It is a beautiful engineering masterpiece.

The Straits of Mackinac, up to this time, was crossed by Ferry Boat, which took about 45 minutes. The bridge saved travelers time and money in crossing the Straits. No more long lines to wait in for an available ferry. This did wonders for the tourist trade in the Upper Peninsula.

THE SIXTIES

My other three grandchildren, Leonard, Loren and Lisa were born during these years. While all five grandchildren were small, they took turns spending the night and going places with Grandpa and Grandma. Also there were the reading to, telling stories, playing games, playing the piano and singing. We enjoyed taking them places. Barbara sent them to us clean and neat and they were very well behaved. There is usually a very good relationship between grandparents and grandchildren. Lloyd and Barbara live close enough to us so that we have and still do see them often. The lane on our farm goes near enough to their home so there was no need to travel the roadway.

Census Taker — Enumerator

Even unto this day some people have not taken too kindly to answering some of the necessary questions asked by the U.S. Census Bureau. This can cause trouble for the enumerator. It is a necessary part of government.

In biblical times, the count of the people, as well as securing some other necessary information, was found to be helpful for the good of the country.

The first United States Census was taken in 1790 and it has been taken every ten years since. This first Bureau of the Census was later transferred to the Department of the Interior and is written into the United States Constitution.

The census takers or enumerators are selected by the political party in office at the time. Eisenhower was president. George Slaght was supervisor of Mundy Township and I was a Republican. George was looking for possible census takers. He suggested that I try for the job.

It is necessary to write and pass a civil service test and to have certain character qualifications. One would be selected by members of the local census board as there were supposed to be more applicants than were needed. If chosen, you would be given a certain geographic area to work and a designated length of time to complete the work.

My supervisor said to me, "We know more about you than you know about yourself."

We traveled about thirty-five miles to Howell to get our instructions. The farm census was taken first followed soon by the population census. I happened to be selected for both. One had to follow a similar pattern for each assignment. I knew that a few people were "touchy" about being asked personal questions and would be likely to throw the caller out. We were supposed to do a one hundred percent job. I succeeded with my territory and was asked to try and get a few in other areas who had so far "rebelled." I happened to be successful there too.

I went prepared by taking my text book "Government of the United States." When necessary I would show them where it was written into the constitution.

Some of these events took place in my own area. Others were the toughies from other areas.

First, I listened to them; letting me know how they felt about "this business." Getting it out of their system was important and seemed to provide a safety valve.

Things usually went fairly smooth from there on. Here are a few of my experiences as a census taker.

A farmer said, "Yes, I will cooperate and answer questions. The last time the census was taken, I was one of those smart alecs who didn't have to and I wasn't going to. Well the authorities caught up with me. When someone says they don't, it is just not so."

As this event took place near the beginning of my work, I asked if I might use his experience but not his name. He gave me permission. I used the information but have never squealed on him.

One neighbor said, "If I had have known what you were here for I would not have opened the door." Reluctantly they gave me the necessary information.

These people were strangers. This man just didn't do anything that he didn't want to do. I left, but by the next morning I had figured out a plan and called back. Explaining the first man's experience I didn't want him to get into trouble too. Maybe I hadn't been clear enough. I was very concerned that I hadn't fulfilled my duty. I didn't want to feel responsible for causing him to get into any legal entanglement.

Immediately his wife came forth with, "We will answer the questions."

The next household had been called on before, harsh words had been spoken and the enumerator was unsuccessful. Hence, he wasn't happy with me. His language was vulgar and uncouth. He seemed to be out of step with the whole world. At this time his mother-in-law was also staying in their home. This made his expenses high and especially for her extra food and so on and on. Finally, his wife, who couldn't stand it any longer, took over. I received the information and he mellowed somewhat.

The final difficult case was with a lady who had been called on previously. She was really furious, to begin with and shook her fist in my face. I listened, she cooled down, invited me into the house and answered the questions. She showed me her pretty treasured articles including her own hand painted china and acted as if she was ashamed of herself. She also invited me to visit her where she worked, which was at the Dort House on East Kearsley Street, Flint. I wasted no time in accepting that invitation as I had always admired that house and had never visited many rich people's homes.

Mardi Gras

Walter had another hernia operation and about a year later, he got dentures. During this time while he was recuperating from his surgery we took a trip to New Orleans to the Mardi Gras. We got a motel room and left our car about 30 miles away, towards Baton Rouge. We took a bus to the center of the Mardi Gras area and had a very exciting day. The next two days we toured the city, St. Marin's and the delta area. I had wondered where the telephone and electric companies got all of those tall straight poles, but driving the length of the state of Mississippi from north to south on this trip, I knew. That is where those tall straight trees grew.

Decorated House

We completely painted and papered the inside of our house and laid a new wall-to-wall wool carpet. Howard Stiff and his grandson from Linden did the decorating. Dean Merritt from Skaff's laid the carpet. Each was very skilled at his profession. Dean, soon after that, coincidentally, bought a lot on the back of our property and built a home.

Coats

I had nerve enough to make an off-white spring coat. That was so successful that I bought blue-gray wool material and made a winter coat. Clyde Burtrum, of Burtrum Furs in Flint, matched gray mink fur for a collar. I sort of felt like a strutting peacock. With the material I had left plus a little more from the Herbert N. Bush Store where I had bought the original material, I made my granddaughter Cindy a very pretty coat. She was five years old and very proud to have a coat like Grandma's, but the white rabbit fur collar had to be removed because it frightened her! I fashioned a scarf made from the coat material to take its place.

Myers-Somers Genealogy

Helen Griggs died in the early 1950's. Her parents came here from New York state the same as my grandmother did in about 1870. She had put together a very complete genealogy book; she had begun working on it in about 1910. The family had given it to Alice Heermann Berlin, who was a cousin to Helen, to work with and protect. Up until this time, all that I knew about my ancestors was who the immediate families were. I studied this book intently and then in 1964, we visited the Schoharie County area in New York which is close to Green County where some of Walter's cousins live. We found some of my cousins who helped me to understand Helen's book.

My cousin in Grand Blanc suggested that while Walter and I were in Schoharie County, we contact George and Harriet Collins in Seward, New York. As we stopped in Sharon at a service station to inquire about Seward and if they knew the Collins', he said, "Yes," and pointed us toward Collins' place of employment. We were able to catch him before he left for home.

We stayed with them and they took us around to visit other cousins.

One of them gave us the name of William Summers of Billings, Montana, who had been doing extensive research on the family and had included my name on some of his genealogy charts. I became acquainted with him and his wife Doreen and visited them in 1965. They visited us in 1966 and again in 1978. During that time, I was able to assist him by furnishing missing information for his records.

The original Somers family was from Frankfort, Germany. The first Somers to come to America was Peter Nicholas Somers who was from Frankfort and was sent to New York as a Lutheran missionary.

Bill Summers went to Frankfort and searched records to trace back four more generations to the year 1575.

In 1979, Bill sent me a complimentary copy of his book titled "Somers, Sommers, Sommer and Summers Who Missed the Boat." He published a beautiful, well-arranged book complete with pictures, stories, name charts and indexes covering over four centuries of our family genealogy.

I am of the seventh generation of the Peter Somers family.

St. Lawrence Seaway

This had been a long-talked-about project and a long time under construction. In 1962, the St. Lawrence River Seaway was opened to traffic from Duluth in Minnesota to the Atlantic Ocean, between Canada and the United States, a distance of 2,687 miles. This provided a commercial outlet to the world markets for produce of the middle western states.

Vietnam War

This turned out to be a long drawn-out war. It was unsuccessful, sad, and no-win. The soldiers who served there were not honored like other service men had been. Perhaps they suffered more. People as a whole were not as patriotic as usual. It was considered a failure with so many lives lost and so much money spent.

Assassination

In November 1963, President John F. Kennedy was assassinated in Dallas, Texas. The news traveled to everyone so quickly that it left us all in a state of shock. We were on our way home from a visit to Canada and we were just west of Port Huron when we stopped at a restaurant. As we entered there was such a silence that we wondered what the trouble was. The waitress who waited on us leaned down and said to us, "Kennedy has been shot." This was something that most of the people living at this time never expected to happen. It saddened not only the United States but the whole world.

Spacecraft

At this time, spacecraft was coming into being and was very successful. Men were now traveling into space, circling the earth and landing safely. In 1969, man made a safe landing on the moon, spent time there and returned safely to earth. Everyone was glued to the TV to watch these fantastic accomplishments as they were in progress. We all wondered if it could really be done.

Change in Farming

The Mitchell Bros. were getting to the stage where they wanted less hustle. Cecil Mitchell, George's son, handled the dairy for about a year. The system was now changing, and we would have to invest quite a sum of money to modernize our dairy outfit for the changeover as well as invest much more work and have less free time. Consequently, we went out of dairy and into crop farming and fed about 25 head of beef cattle.

We also got out of the chicken business.

The grocery market we had been supplying poultry and eggs to went out of business and in order for us to find a new market we would have had to modernize this end of the farm, too.

New York City — 1965

Annie Gunn, Walter's cousin, who lives in Toronto, Ontario, Canada, and I visited New York City for about eleven days in May 1965. We traveled by bus. We visited all the places of interest and had a few experiences that tourists don't usually get because Annie had a friend there. The first thing we did was to take a boat ride around Manhattan. That is the way to get places located. We went up the Empire State Building as high as possible. The view was "ever so far." We saw the United Nations Building, Ellis Island, the Statue of Liberty, Macy's, Wall Street, Greenwich Village, and the World's Fair in Flushing, New York.

Our most unusual experience was visiting millionaires' quarters on 5th Avenue across from Central Park. We were near the Jackie Kennedy Onassis and Peter Lawford homes. A friend of Annie's, an Irish lady, worked as a maid for these people. They lived in a high-rise apartment complex which was very lavish. This friend had told us how to get there and when to come so that she could have some time to spend with us and have dinner for us in between her duties.

This was like visiting two different worlds. We approached the front entrance, were met by a stiff, uniformed and white-gloved doorman. He wanted to know who we wanted to see. He said to wait a few minutes until another man came on duty and he was out of uniform, then he would take us to see the Irish maid. As we were waiting (I think outside), we could see the elegant receiving room and elevator. When he came for us, we went to the back of the building and took the hinky-dinky freight elevator to the eighth floor to the servants' quarters, which were also hinky-dinky. There were, I think, three tiny rooms for three maids, with lumpy single beds, an uncomfortable rocking chair, small dresser, tiny window, closet, one small bathroom and a small area with a table and chairs for dining, which was not at all attractive.

There was a huge well-equipped kitchen with several beautiful sets of dishes, silver, crystal and all of the lovely items needed for serving dinners to many people. Between the kitchen and the owner's beautiful quarters was a lovely silk folding screen for the serving maid to pass around when serving dinners. Annie and I had a chance to view this area. There were gold, marble, satin, lace, mahogany, all types of chandeliers, huge and small, in the fourteen foot ceilings and on side walls. Windows and doors reached the ceiling. Cleaners came in twice a year to shine the chandeliers. They shined them with ammonia, and they sure did sparkle. Here you could see two worlds just by peeking around a silk folding screen.

As we visited, we learned that it was becoming difficult to find this kind of help for very wealthy people. About the only people who would work for these millionaires came from the European countries, and they were catching on fast. They soon learned that it would be nicer to have weekends and holidays off instead of a few hours some afternoons and occasionally an evening after the work was finished and the dog was walked. At that time the average salary was about $175.00 per month plus their living expenses.

After I had returned home and was telling and complaining about this to Walter, I said, "That fancy and seemingly idle life was not for me."

He said, "Then you would rather keep house for Walt?"

I replied, "I sure would." It was a once in a lifetime experience that was valuable to me.

Lauris (Baum) Mallory

It was about a thirty minute bus ride from Port Authority Station to Upper Montclair, New Jersey, where we visited a relative of mine whom I had never seen but had corresponded with. Lauris Mallory and Helen Griggs had exchanged valuable genealogy information about the Somers families back around 1910 and later when they were young ladies. They never met, but they did a marvelous job by correspondence. Due to their information, William Summers, Billings, Montana, was grateful for so much information for his genealogy book during the 1960's and the 1970's.

Long Island

Annie Gunn had another friend who lived about 85 miles out on Long Island, New York. We took a plush train from Pennsylvania Station in Manhattan under the Hudson River to Jamaica. There we changed to a dowdy train and a very rough track, with very few passengers to reach their home. The countryside was mostly potato and duck farms and duck and potato farms. They were prosperous looking farms and homes.

We visited all of the places that regular tourists visit plus the World's Fair in Flushing, New York, and also all the amusing things that we did by knowing the right people. It was a very exciting trip.

Henry and Laila Rohloff

Henry and Laila Rohloff lived in the Goodrich area. Laila and I had become acquainted while attending Genesee County Normal School in 1917 and 1918. We had kept in touch and had taken a few short trips together.

In 1965, she retired from teaching. That summer we took our first long trip together. We went to the west coast by a northern route visiting people and interesting places such as: Yellowstone National Park, Mt. Rushmore, Bad Lands in the Dakotas, Glacier National Park, some of the big dams and Washington and Oregon forests. We drove along the Pacific Coast of Oregon and California, through the Redwoods, hopped over into Mexico, Arizona, Petrified Forest, Grand Canyon, etc.

As we came through Oklahoma, we wanted to see if we could locate Loren McGarvin, the young man who had worked for us in 1923–24. All that we knew of his whereabouts was that he had grown up in a little town a short distance south of Chickasaw. We inquired in many places and after much seeking, we found him in Anadarka, Oklahoma. He had had some strokes and his eyesight was failing. It was a happy meeting after all of these years. His wife (part Indian) is a very nice person and made us welcome.

This area is subject to sudden storms and tornadoes. Most people have storm shelters. Theirs is well stocked and I guess, used often. When the warning comes — you GO! — DON'T WAIT! A warning came while we were visiting there. We were all hustled into their shelter. There were nine adults, a baby and a dog. It was crowded and hot in there. The storm was quite severe but didn't last long. This was a new experience for us. We visited them twice before Loren died.

This trip took five and one-half weeks and was well worth the time and money.

In 1967 we traveled with Henry and Laila again.

We went east through Canada along the St. Lawrence Seaway, Massena, Locks, Thousand Islands, "Montreal Expo," and area, Quebec and home through Maine, New Hampshire, Vermont and New York State at the time of the beautiful fall color.

1968 — County Normal Anniversary

1968 was the 50th Anniversary of my graduation from Genesee County Normal School in June 1918. I also started teaching at the Kline School in September 1918. Both groups were having yearly gatherings. It just happened that we were entertaining both groups about two or three weeks apart. I happened to think about this being the 50th Anniversary for each group. I planned and decorated for each event. None of them had given this a thought. It was a happy surprise for all.

WALTER AND EDNA MITCHELL

On their Golden Wedding Anniversary Day

THE SEVENTIES

During the month of May, 1970, Erma and I visited England, Scotland and Iceland. We flew by Pan Am from Metro Detroit to London in a little less than seven hours and set our watches ahead six hours. We spent a few days in London before setting out for the countryside and visiting our relatives.

London, England

In London all taxis are black. Buses are double-deckers and are red. We rode the bus and taxi and took a private taxi tour. Our driver was about five years old when Germany bombshelled London and had spent most of his young life in bomb shelters. Needless to say he was a very interesting person to talk to. In England, he was working toward his own taxi service and he had to apprentice for two years. He was a young man and was an excellent guide. He had grown up during the rebuilding after the war and was very knowledgeable about London. He answered many questions for us and showed us many places we never would have thought to ask about; places that were not included on public tours.

Some of the places we visited were so located that we walked to them. We visited Regent Street, Big Ben, Piccadilly Circus, the Parliament buildings, Westminster Abbey, St. Paul's Cathedral, and #10 Downing St.

Following are some of the other interesting things we saw and did on our visit in London. We attended the theater and saw "Charlie Girl," a musical comedy. We also visited "Charles Dickens' Old Curiosity Shop." We went to the Tower of London and to Buckingham Palace where we viewed the Changing of the Guard and the Horse Guard. We saw the Yeomen, and the Warders (Beefeaters) wearing colorful uniforms. Erma and I had our picture taken with one of them.

Soapbox Parliament or Speaker's Corner is located in Hyde Park and that was a unique place to pass by. People can go there and express their views on any topic without fear of being persecuted.

We next toured the Kew Gardens and then took a boat ride down the Thames.

Nine Days With an English Car

Erma had the use of a small English General Motors car for nine days as she is an employee of General Motors in Lansing, Michigan. The cars were very small.

England is small; the roads are narrow with high hedges on either side and very sharp, short corners, which are very close to peoples' buildings. We saw some people pick up the rear end of a car and hoist it around a corner.

The man with our car came and picked us up at our hotel and drove us near an entrance to Motorway M4. He was to give Erma instructions, as the English drive on the opposite side of the road and this was confusing to us. As he was about to give the car over to us, a wire underneath the car caught the brake and quicker than a wink, it flipped us completely around and

```
"NUMBER FIVE"                      PROPRIETORS :
STRATFORD ROAD                 L. N. PRIOR, A. J. TEDMAN
SHIPSTON-ON-STOUR
WARWICKSHIRE


              BED, BREAKFAST

                     AND

              EVENING MEAL


        Tel. SHIPSTON-ON-STOUR 367
```

stopped. He kept it from turning over, maybe going over an embankment and just missed being hit by a big truck (called a lorry in England). He then let us take his company car which was a little bit bigger car. Erma handled it very well.

We headed west and stopped at Windsor Castle. We couldn't seem to find a good parking place. We took a chance and parked in a spot where we were not sure we should be while visiting the Castle and when we came out, you guessed it; we had a two pound traffic ticket for illegal parking.

Bed and Breakfast

There are many small towns throughout the countryside. None of them have big stores, just small shops which carry one line of merchandise, such as a bakery, a drug store, a meat market and so on. Neither do they have any motels or hotels. Private homes have signs, "Bed and Breakfast." They are nice and comfortable places to stay, the food is delicious and there is so much of

ANCESTRAL HOME OF THE KNILL FAMILY

In the village of Braunton, North Devonshire. The author is on the left with Nellie Lamprey, a niece of Edna's grandmother.

it. We were on our way to North Devonshire, to the western part near the Atlantic Ocean, to the small town of Braunton.

This area is where my grandparents lived before they came to Michigan. We found our cousin Nellie Lamprey, who was about six years older than I am, her brother William, and another cousin Phyllis Hill, who lived in Barnstable. We visited the house where my great grandparents had lived, their church, church-yard, the cemetery and their gravestones.

Cousin Nellie went with us to St. Ives, Cornwall and Land's End. We then went back east to Plymouth where the Pilgrims embarked for America, then to Exeter to visit Nellie's brother Alfred, his wife, and their two daughters and their husbands, and their two sons. Alfred and I had corresponded when we were

BURIAL GROUNDS

Of English forebearers James Richard Knill and Elizabeth Davis Knill, in yard of St. Brannock's Church, Braunton.

young. He spent his life in the English Army and was stationed in India when we were in touch with one another.

Our trip was properly timed. Within two years, Nellie, William, Alfred and his wife had all passed away.

Shakespearian Country

As we left Devonshire, we drove east and north through the beautiful countryside to Shakespearian Country, the Stratford on Avon Theater, and saw the play "Measure for Measure." We visited Trinity Church Chapel, the Susanna Shakespeare Home, and the Mary Arden and Anne Hathaway Homes. England is a beautiful country, especially in this area and in the month of May.

Thatched Roofs

Thatched roofs were popular many, many years ago. As other material became available, less expensive and less of a fire hazard, thatching was discontinued. This type of roof has been making a comeback since 1967. There is a requirement to preserve those good ones in existence, because very few people know the art. Thatching in England is not only an art, it is a science. The best thatched roof in England is made of Norfolk reed which comes from the marshes of eastern England. For an average five-room house, the cost is nearly $2,000.00 and will last about 70 years. The next best material is wheat reed or Devon reed, which will cost about $1,000.00 and will last about 35 years. Straw thatch will last 15 or 20 years and costs about $600.00. This thatch is laid about 12 inches thick at a 45 degree angle. Heavy rain will only penetrate about one-fourth to one-half inch if properly laid. They are now fire-proofing and putting something like chicken wire over these thatched roofs to protect them from wind, birds and small animals.

Dover

We are now back in London without the car. We took a bus to Dover. The buses and trains are very clean, comfortable and sightly. I guess the people use them more than we Yankees do ours, so they can afford to keep their public transportation in good condition. In the United States we enjoy our own cars and nearly everyone has one. That is not the way it is in other countries.

I was very anxious to see the White Cliffs of Dover and I was not disappointed. They were beautiful!

Hovercraft Ride

Air can take the place of wheels, tracks and hulls. The Hovercraft uses propellers and an air cushion that inflates and deflates. It loads and unloads on land. It carries heavy loads and travels at a high rate of speed. It skims along just above the water and it is a very smooth and pleasant ride. Erma and I rode across the English Channel from Dover to Boulogne, France, stayed a few hours, then returned to Dover. It was unique to us.

Scotland

We traveled by train from London to Edinburgh, Scotland, which took about six hours through very scenic countryside. We spent a few days there visiting such places as Edinburgh Castle, Princess St., the Sir Walter Scott Monument, flower gardens and a glass factory. We took a bus trip through the countryside visiting Loch Lomond and Trossachs, Ben Lomond, Loch Katrine, Ben Ledi, Callander and Stirling.

Peebles

Peebles is a small city about 25 miles south of Edinburgh. A friend gave us a nice tour of that area. This is where the Alexander Scott Family came from to Canada. They are ancestors of my mother-in-law, Agnes Penny Mitchell. They were printers and there we found the original printing shop which is still being used.

A SCOTCH HIGHLAND COW AND CALF

The likes of which we saw often along the countryside of Scotland.

Glasgow

We left Edinburgh by bus for Glasgow, but we didn't see much of Glasgow. We soon left by Icelandair to Iceland, which was about a three hour ride. We bused to Reykjavik, about a 45 minute ride from the airport.

Iceland

Iceland is a small country, about 200 miles by 300 miles. The population is about 200,000, living mostly in the southwestern area. Reykjavik is the largest city, having a population of 85,000

A FAIR SAMPLE
OF THE PRODUCE OF ICELAND.

or more. The country was formed by volcanos. The lava forms good roadbeds as well as productive soil. It is almost a treeless country, although there is much experimenting with trees at the present time.

There are many hot springs in the Reykjavik area. The boiling water and steam are piped, stored and used, especially to heat homes and other buildings. There are no chimneys on the buildings. There is one public outdoor swimming pool that is used all winter. They are experimenting with indoor tropical fruits and plants which should thrive in the environment of the hot springs.

A GREEN GROWING TURF ROOF

On a coastal plain, near Reykjavik.

Turf Roof

Many years ago the sod roofs, which were soil and grass roots, were used on most of the buildings. This was discontinued. Few are being preserved. The few we saw were alive. They were a pretty shade of green and as neatly trimmed as a lawn.

Live Volcano

We rode a bus from Reykjavik from 5:00 p.m. until 3:30 a.m., about 70 miles east into the mountains to view a volcano which had been erupting for about ten days. At that time of the year, the sun was shining nearly all of the 24 hours. I would say that it was dusk, not dark, from about 2:00 a.m. until about 4:00 a.m.

We rode through the farming country. Marshlands had been drained into grasslands. The average farm had about 100 acres, with 15 dairy cows and about 200 sheep. The farm buildings were comfortable and neat looking. There were a few small silos and some light farm machinery. They raised wheat, corn and had lots of hay.

The southwestern part of the country is warmed by the Gulf Stream. The lowlands in this area do not have extreme weather conditions.

As we approached the erupting area, the bus stopped a safe distance away. People could go a little closer by walking or taking a jeep. Erma walked and I took a jeep. We were still a safe distance away but close to the cooled lava coming from within the earth. There were loud and heavy roars. Fire and pieces of lava were shooting hundreds of feet into the air. It was pushing, shoving, crunching and moving great distances. It was forming great new high ridged mounds as it cooled, and became solid and hard. A man picked up some small pieces which were still quite hot. He gave me a few pieces about the size of golf balls. When they cooled, they became black, porous and not very heavy. I still have them as well as a few pieces of rock from a hot spring.

Trade

They have only two main products to export in Iceland. One is woolen products that they make from the many sheep they raise.

Fishing is the other important industry, especially the dried fish, which is accomplished by hanging it on racks outdoors. Due to perfect weather conditions and lack of flies and insects, it is an ideal and inexpensive method of preserving their fish for exporting.

Nearly everything else they use has to be imported.

Crime

The Icelanders scarcely know what crime is. They don't know about rich and poor. They are well educated and well read. Nearly all are hardworking and thrifty people. If there is a need, the government handles the situation.

Saturday night is their night on the town at hotels and other gathering places. A few get drunk. These are put in jail for the night to sober up and let out. The remainder of the time, the few jails that they have are empty.

Horses

Small horses seem to have been in the country since it was inhabited. They are so well-adapted and so efficient for the peoples' needs that they do not allow any other horses to come into the country. They don't want any part of cross-breeding as that would eliminate the original native horse in time.

Home Flight

The flight back to New York City was very picturesque, especially when flying over the Greenland glaciers while the sun was shining on them. The pilot drew our attention to them and informed us when to take pictures.

House Decorating — 1971

After another ten years, it was time for another house decorating, including upholstering our two-piece davenport and three chairs. My friend Mary Selden's brother and wife, Glen and Norene Collins, did the decorating for us. They did very nice work. I liked to have the complete job done all at one time. This saved having your home torn up for an extended period like doing things piecemeal does.

Coats

I was so happy with my 1960's coats that I did a repeat and made two coats again in 1971. I have always made all of my own clothes. I usually have in mind what I need and find it easier to shop for material to make it than to try to find it ready-made.

Father Died

Fred Holland, my father, was nearly 95 years old when he died, March 31, 1972, after a few days of illness. He had lived an active and busy life. He had been still driving his car in a limited way, doing a few carpenter jobs, living in his own home and handling his own business. He lived in a commendable life style to the very last.

Walter's 75th Birthday

Walter's 75th birthday was August 21, 1973. I arranged a surprise party for him. The guests were Emery and Julia Gudith, Willard and Alice Harris, Tom Mitchell and Amon Berlin. I had tickets to Whiting Auditorium to see the play "South Pacific."

While we were gone, Erma and Lloyd's family came in and prepared a lavish dinner. The cars were hidden and the house looked as if there was no one around. We entered the house and were greeted by—SURPRISE!

Golden Wedding Anniversary

On September 26, 1973, Walter and I had been married 50 years. We had a big celebration at the Mundy Township Hall in Rankin. For the next week or so, a few small groups of people came to the house, those who were unable to come to the celebration. In all we entertained about 300 people. It was a gala affair.

Alaska

As a finishing off of our Golden Wedding celebration, we planned a trip to Alaska, June 25–July 17, 1974. We engaged a travel agency in Sarnia to make the arrangements for our own trip, as we were to be traveling through Canada.

The Rev. B.J. Holcomb, a former pastor of South Mundy United Methodist Church, and his wife Illah were then living in Traverse City and traveled with us. We were a very compatible foursome.

We left our car with Walter's cousins, Sarah Passingham and Marion and Jack Wilton, near Sarnia.

We took the day train from Sarnia to Toronto. From there we took the sleeper train by the northern route to Edmonton. This was a new experience for all of us. We were very excited about living on a train for a few days. We had a bedroom with bunk beds, toilet, sink and shower. In the morning they folded our bed, and we had easy chairs. Our sleeping quarters became our living room. At night our bed was made for us. We ate our meals in the dining car. We were waited on hand and foot as we viewed the passing scenery in luxury.

We toured Edmonton, then took a bus through the Fraser

Valley for a two day ride through that beautiful countryside and crossed the Continental Divide on our way to Vancouver.

We spent a few days there and in Victoria, taking tours, including Butchart Gardens.

We spent the first evening in Vancouver with Erma. She was on another tour coming back from Alaska by boat to Vancouver on her way home. We were each spending the night there and our hotels were only a few blocks apart. Before leaving home, we were looking over each other's agenda and discovered this very unusual happening. We then planned to spend the evening together. This was something that never would have worked out if we had tried to plan it that way!

Our ship was the "Spirit of London." This was a four day trip up the inside passage as far as Skagway. We were supposed to take a narrow guage railway up through the Yukon to Whitehorse. There was a bridge out. The train could not make the run.

We made many stops along the way, such as in Ketchikan, Menden Hall glacier, Juneau, Haines and Sitka. We boated through Glacier Bay, were fairly close to glaciers, icebergs and seals, then back to Vancouver after spending eight days on the ship.

We boarded the sleeping train on the Southern Canadian Route, through Banff-Calgary back to Toronto, Sarnia and home. It was a deluxe trip.

Walter's Illness

Soon after we returned home from the Alaska trip, Walter went into the hospital. It was discovered that he had leukemia. The condition was soon regulated. The treatment didn't cause him too much discomfort. He lived a fairly normal life. However, his system was unable to fight off infection, so occasionally he would go into the hospital for a few days.

In 1979, Fred, Erma, Scott, Walter and I took a trip to the southeast. It was very, very hot. Walter went into the hospital in

Richmond, Virginia for about two weeks. As soon as he was able, we came home without finishing the trip.

1975 Birthday

March 8, 1975 was my 75th birthday. The family gave me a nice party at my home. It was a happy occasion with many relatives and friends present.

1976

This was the United States Bicentennial Celebration. It was an event to be proud of. I think that Michigan had one of, or maybe the most attractive auto license plates of any of the states. I saved ours and have it shined and hanging in my kitchen.

Erma Weds

On July 2, 1976, Erma and Fred Parks, both living in Lansing, were married in the South Mundy United Methodist Church by the Rev. T. Thornley Eddy, the reception being in our home for about 65 guests. They spent a few days at Niagara Falls, New York.

My Illness — 1976

I have had but few illnesses during my lifetime. In November, I had a double operation at one time, the removal of my gall bladder and kidney stones. This sickness came onto me suddenly. It took most of the winter to recover, but I have been very well since. It is now January 1984.

Tides and Helicopters — 1977

Erma, Fred, Scott (Fred's son), Walter and I went through our eastern states, to New Brunswick and Nova Scotia and Prince Edward Island and home through Canada along the St. Lawrence River, Quebec, Montreal, and Toronto. My highlight was to see the Tidal Bore. This was very spectacular at Saint John and Moncton in New Brunswick. The tide comes rushing into the Bay of Fundy, which is a narrow body of water. There is an enormous amount of water and speed. The riverbeds will be nearly dry except for a few potholes. The water will rise five to six feet in a very few minutes. The rivers will back up, flowing upstream into the countryside for miles and miles. This area and Western England are the two places where I have seen such spectacular and almost unbelievable tides.

The five of us took another trip to tour some of the western states.

For some time, I had been wanting a helicopter ride. I don't know why; I guess I like some adventure now and then. We were in St. Louis, Missouri, near the Gateway Arch. People were being taken for helicopter rides. Scott Parks and I took a ride over the city of St. Louis. It was a thrill, very sightly and a rich experience.

China Cabinet

For some time I had wanted a china cabinet with a light to display my hand-painted china and glassware. Finally, we "broke down" and bought a very pretty one from Ethan Allen's in Grand Blanc. It is a compliment to my home.

THE EIGHTIES

Walter had been living with the leukemia for about seven years with some ups and downs. His life had been quite normal for a man of his age. He went into the hospital the last of February. He died in his sleep on March 3, 1980. He was eighty one and one-half years of age. We had been married fifty six and one-half years.

Books

I started a Phobia-Hang up Collection about February 1, 1980. Bruce and Barbara Mitchell happened to be spending the evening with us. A fire truck or ambulance went speeding past with its siren blasting. Bruce is bothered by the sound of a siren. It winds him up. As it happened, we found out by discussing the subject that each of us had a phobia or hang up. The next morning I was all lit up and inspired to write a book. I began having visitors write a page in my notebook about their personal hang ups. It worked so well and was so successful that by Labor Day of that year, I started another notebook of my friends recounting of

227

their blunders or goofs. These are fun books and they give me a chance to meet people.

Barn Roof — Paint

I had a new roof put on one of the barns and all of the buildings were painted by Carl Minnett. He was a neighbor who did odd jobs for us for a number of years and did very good work.

Caribbean Cruise

Erma, Fred, Scott and I spent a week on a Caribbean Cruise sponsored by the National Guard. We flew from Metro Airport, Detroit to New York City and on to San Juan. At this point, we took a ship and visited these islands: Barbadoes, St. Lucia, Guadeloupe, Antiqua, St. Thomas and back to San Juan for our flight back to New York City, then to Detroit and home. We had stopped at each island long enough to take a tour and see how the people live. There are many poor people but they seem quite contented, as their needs are few and their lives are relaxed. They lead a much slower-paced simpler life than we do.

St. Thomas is a prosperous place, having expensive shopping areas, homes, clubs, and water activities. We had the pleasure of visiting our neighbors Tom and Pat O'Conner's beautiful vacation home on a mountainside there.

Dallas, Texas

Mary McDowell, a friend of my daughter Erma (they both worked in Lansing), was driving to Dallas to visit her family. She asked me to go along as a traveling companion.

I visited Jewell Loftin in Fort Worth who was our neighbor for twenty years on Grand Blanc Road. We were gone over Christmas and New Year's. It is the only time that I ever spent the holidays away from my family. I will mention a few unusual happenings.

I spent Christmas Day and New Year's Eve with one Catholic, one Jew, four Moslems, three Methodists and a "people dog." This dog was treated like a person and never caused a speck of trouble.

I would like to tell you about my experience as a captive baby sitter. I was resting in a plaza waiting for my friends who were Christmas shopping, when along came a strange man with a huge bag of Christmas presents and a boy and girl about eight and nine years old. He asked if I would be sitting there for a while and if I would watch the children and the presents. He was gone for quite some time, then came to check if all was going well and off he went again. The next time he came back, he had his wife and more presents. They took the presents and children and away they went. I enjoyed the children. The family had recently moved to Dallas from Colorado, seeking work. Maybe there are advantages to being elderly, looking trustworthy and not being able to make a quick get-away!

We went to an art gallery in Dallas where they had a Bronze Age exhibit of Chinese artifacts used by a civilization dated between 2000 and 4000 B.C. It was most interesting. Five cities in the United States displayed these artifacts during the year. We happened to be there when they were shown in Dallas. They were beautiful and well preserved.

Here, being elderly again proved helpful to me. I never was very efficient at standing in long lines. A wheelchair was available for the so-called infirm. It was secured for me. I was then seated inside the gallery to wait for my party as they came through. This was first-class.

This aforementioned small black dog owned by Mary McDowell made the entire trip with us and was the source of curiosity and entertainment. After a two-week stay we were finally packing the car for our homeward journey. All at once this little black dog came up missing. We searched the premises high and low looking for the rascal. Finally, we gave up and went back to finish the packing of the car. Lo and behold, there he was in his prepared raised riding position between the bucket seats waiting patiently for us to get going. It was evident that this dog was very intelligent, understood our intentions and thus knew our every move.

President Wounded

President Ronald Reagan was shot and seriously wounded on March 30, 1981, along with two other men. That was a big shock to the nation. It does not seem possible that such things can happen, but they do. He recovered quite soon and seems not to have suffered any lingering after effects.

Columbia Space Shuttle — 1981

The Columbia Space Shuttle was the first shuttle to be returned to earth. It landed safely in April of 1981 after having circled the earth thirty-six times.

On November 28, 1983, the Columbia was sent aloft again carrying the new one billion dollar Spacelab Research Station. A crew of six on a nine-day mission conducted dozens of experiments using a 23 foot long reusable orbital laboratory. Spacelab was developed and built by ten European nations and given to the United States as Western Europe's contribution to the American Space Transportation System.

Gardening

A neighbor and friend, Madge Billsbrough, had gardened with me for about thirty years. We both liked raising our own food and the work that went with it, such as: canning, freezing, pickling, kraut making and raising pretty flowers. She died in December, 1981, after a few months illness.

Nan Rahn, our minister's wife, gardened with me in 1982–83. She didn't know anything about gardening but caught on fast and was a very good worker. She was also a very good kraut maker. Madge had taught her.

This is the recipe they used for sauerkraut: Remove core and outside leaves from solid heads of cabbage. Shred cabbage fairly fine. To every five pounds of shredded cabbage, add three table-spoons of coarse pickling salt. Tap gently to settle the salt and to extract the juice from the cabbage. When finished there should be enough juice to cover the cabbage. Put a piece of wrap over the kraut and then place a plastic bag filled with water on top of the cabbage to keep out the air and to weight down the cabbage until it has thoroughly fermented. It will take a few weeks before it will be ready. Then you can or freeze it. (If you freeze it you don't have to cook it first.) August is a good time to make it. It ferments quicker in warm weather. I think it is more appetizing.

Ferris Wheel

Erma, Fred, his daughter Karen, and I visited Niagara Falls during Memorial Day weekend. A new amusement park had been built near the Falls. They had a huge ferris wheel, one of the newest and the highest ones ever built. The ferris wheel was always one of my favorite rides. I was anxious to ride and really enjoyed it. We were in the area again in the fall of 1983. I took another ride then which was just as much fun as the first one.

Globe Trotter

Walter and I had called our daughter Erma a globe trotter. Now her husband Fred seems to enjoy traveling as well. They have been very generous in taking Walter and I with them. Now they still take me. Apparently, we travel well together. I will try to continue to make it pleasant so they won't get disgusted and leave me home.

Westward Ho!

Fred, Erma, Pat Kelley (a friend of Erma's), and I went west. We drove through and visited: Illinois, Iowa, South Dakota, Bad Lands, Black Hills, Mt. Rushmore, Casper, Wyoming (visited my granddaughter, Cindy, who is now home after having been away for about four years), Yellowstone National Park, Billings, Montana (where we visited William and Doreen Summers who wrote the Summers Geneology book), Salt Lake City, Denver, Anadarka, Oklahoma, St. Louis, Indianapolis and I-69, home.

We made the usual circular trip which covered several thousand miles and ended right where we started—at home.

September 1, 1983

Korean Airlines Flight 007 was shot down by Soviet Missiles over the Sea of Japan, killing all 269 people; this horrible disaster shocked the world. Repercussions in international affairs will not soon disappear.

Northeastern Color Trip

Fred, Erma, Pat Kelley and I went east through Canada, Buffalo, Letchworth State Park, Corning, Watkins Glen, Cooperstown, Catskill area and Albany, New York. We continued up through Massachusetts to Boston, Plymouth, Concord, and Lexington areas, sightseeing, visiting relatives and friends and admiring the fall colors.

October 22, 1983 — First Grandchild Married

My first grandchild to be married was Leonard Mitchell. He married Amy Mundy on October 22, 1983. They had a very pretty wedding.

Geography

As a child I enjoyed studying geography. I had visions of far away places, countrysides, large cities, mountains, deserts, forests, and oceans. When it comes to luxuries, I am quite a practical person, but if a trip is mentioned, I get into high gear. I am fascinated with large cities and have visited many, but I want no part of living in one. I am a very rural-minded person and that is where I always want to live. I never liked being away from home very long at a time.

Conclusion

For most of the time these following things have been a part of my life: a striking clock, a sewing machine, The Flint Journal newspaper, the telephone, an automobile to drive since I was fifteen, ample food and clothing, and a family of which I am and always can be proud, both before and after my presence here.

It is now January 1984. I am closing my chronological autobiography at this time.

Whatever additional pleasures this life provides for me from here on out, I shall consider as a coupon because I have already enjoyed more than my share.

PREDICTIONS

My predictions for the early years of the twenty-first century are:

1. Spacecraft will serve a useful purpose.
2. Organized labor will have less power.
3. There will be more discipline and respect within the home.
4. Single parent families will become obsolete.
5. Out of necessity, people will shed their extravagant and wasteful habits.
6. Recycling waste materials to conserve resources will become a great industry.
7. There will be neutralization of toxic wastes by chemical methods.
8. Ocean agriculture will be utilized to feed earth's billions with many living under the sea.
9. There will be space colonization.
10. Communication with other beings in the unknown universe will take place.

ADDITIONAL POETRY

ODE TO THE DAYS

'Twas in his youthful days
    A wooin' Sam did go
But all the folks — his affairs
    Were very sure to know.

So by October Nineteen Hundred Five
    Came the day when they were wed
As the preacher, "I now pronounce
    You man and wife," he said.

They, a new and happy
    Household did start
In which, routine and schedule
    Were very much a part.

But some very drastic
    Changes would be due
The arrival of some lively sons
    Yes, there were two.

Now there was a time
    When Sam enjoyed to tease
The neighbor next door would say,
    "Now Sam Day, don't dump my rain barrel, PLEASE!!

To make that better livelihood
    Sam would have to hop
We find him switching
    From railway and mill to shop.

To get his extra sleep and keep things still
    So Mate in this mad rush
Even to the sewing machine
    She'd say, "Sh h h, Hush! Hush!

Sometimes ambitious and
    Venturesome Mate would be
Then we would find her
    Diligently working at the A.C.

For the betterment of neighborhood
    Mate is bound to search
So we find her on a committee
    In the P.T.A., lodge or church

As they reach this, their
    Golden Wedding Year
We extend to them
    Our Best Wishes and Good Cheer.

Written for Sam and Mary Ann Day
    on their Golden Wedding Anniversary.

TRIBUTE TO MARIE WELLS

Many is the time
    The faithful Mrs. Wells
Has tolled for us
    Those joyous morning bells.

All in those
    Eight short years
Filled with many joys
    As well as some few tears.

We have started out
    Our little tots
During which time
    They have grown just lots and lots.

We are glad as can be
    That they on higher levels bent
And most of them
    To higher education went.

And along life's highway
    They view themselves in part
And there it is they find
    Where 'twas they got that start.

Now there comes a time
    When you will leave
But it is not for us
    To sit and grieve.

So as time rolls on
    It's happiness and success for you
And the very best of friends
    That you can hold most true.

As through many hours of bliss
    And the years that swiftly go
It is good old South Mundy
    Who truly loves you so.

Written for the teachers at South Mundy School
    on Mrs. Wells' retirement.

THE LOSS OF A CHILD

Why He takes some of our
    Little Flowers gay
Is not for us to know or say.

Time and time alone can heal
So to Him we do appeal.

To make those heavy hearts more light
As we do know, God's way is right.

MEET AND CHATTER CLUB

In this old world
    Filled with struggle and strife
Our community has tried
    To make for a more abundant life.

Together we would get
    From fifteen to twenty
And have some good times
    There seems to be a plenty.

For us it does seem
    Monotony's no go
It might be a masquerade
    Or perhaps a style show.

Then in the warm summer
    Our families and baskets we take
And off for a picnic
    On the bank of some lake.

Of course we should mention
    The fun we like most
When we hike to the sand hill
    For a good old weiner roast.

When winter is cold
    And evenings are long
We enjoy a nice party
    And perhaps a good song.

Our loyalty, it seems
    Was more strongly built
When we pieced for each other
    A nice friendship quilt.

It adds to our kindness
    When things we exchange
And the articles we find
    Sure cover a wide range.

It might be patterns or recipes
    Or some flowers or seeds
Which help brighten up
    Our home-making needs.

And if it should happen
    That illness or hardship befall
There would be flowers or fruit
    And a nice friendly call.

It wouldn't be right
    Our duties for to shirk
So when Club Day does come
    We just hustle our work.

There are really some things
    That would be much more folly
Than belonging to Our Club
    Which is ever so jolly.

Our lives, it does seem
    We can more closely bind
If the Golden Rule
    We would keep in mind.

CAMPING

'Twas when we were youthful and gay
    An outing we would take
After a careful selection
    It would be—Byram Lake.

It usually would be seven
    Sometimes less, sometimes more
The beds were few and each in turn
    Would sleep upon the floor.

We did enjoy to row and so
    The lake we'd ride about
But it would matter not to us
    The anchor—in or out.

We would just lope and lounge around
    Then to doll up—just so
And wait around impatiently
    For our long looked for BEAU.

The best of things we'd have to eat
    The cupboards we would comb
When packing up our things to take
    As we were leaving home.

Those moonlight rides upon the lake
    Made us so romantic
That Cupid did some changes make
    Those loving hearts did click.

So busy lives and duties bare
    Also a family rear
As many ups and downs we share
    And joys that do appear.

Now many years have passed us by
    And happiness does us bring
As we do get together
    And to these memories cling.

FRIENDS

Some may have the desire to save
    While others would rather spend
But the greatest joy of all is
    To add another friend.

Glory and fame are wonderful
    And a life of — just pretend
But the greatest joy of all
    Is just another friend.

Abundant wealth is very nice
    To royalty — we would bend
Oh! how empty our life would be
    Were we without a friend.

There may be hermits and others
    Who on no one do depend
Much happiness, and world wide good
    They would find in a friend.

Would there be one who would not
    Have a helping hand to lend
When illness or some sorrow befall
    To some very good friend?

Let our lives be full and joyous
    As our way we will wend
Have happiness overflowing
    With many a dear friend.

Some may be beautiful or wise
    While some on strength depends
May I have the ability
    To have just lots of friends.

CONTENTMENT

If for contentment and comfort
    You would want to look
You might find it there
    Between the covers of some book.

Outside it might be
    Oh so dark and dreary
While before the crackling fire
    It is so bright and cheery.

Curled up on the rug
    A purring cat and a slumbering dog
Also are so very happy
    Before the sputtering log.

A very big dish of apples
    Shiny, round and rosy
Now just to settle back
    In your favorite chair so cozy.

Then all fluffy and well buttered
    A heaping dish of corn
Is the satisfaction that
    Into this world you were born.

There are times when for higher things
    Our heart and soul does yearn
Now just to some of your favorite
    Scriptures in the Bible — turn.

So during this lovely dreaming
    These blissful hours do go
Until someone just up and
    Turns on the radio.

When you want to find contentment
    And think you have to roam
You might just try to find it
    In an evening in your home.

SENDING GREETINGS

I find it is so very hard
    To my friends to write a card
It matters not how hard I try
    I'd rather send the card I buy.

So thru the crowds, my way is wrought
    It takes no personal work or thought
To send a little Christmas cheer
    And greetings too throughout the year.

I carefully take last year's list
    Being so sure that none are missed
Hurriedly thru the pile I picked
    And sparingly the stamp I licked.

The pictures and colors are gay
    Words too, if you'd read what you say
Buy them in groups, all just the same
    You don't even have to write your name.

We go thoroughly thru the pile
    Find one written and with a smile
We pick it out, read it o'er and o'er
    And wish that they had written more.

We really make it quite a bore
    And are so glad there are no more
Now wouldn't it be so much better
    Now and then — to write a letter?

IF I HAVE TIME

Sometime I'll do some deeds, that's kind
And the good things I've had in mind,
Our lives will be more closely entwined
    If I have time.

I will not worry, fret or stew
I'll do the things I'd rather do,
There will be smiles and laughter too
    If I have time.

To causes good, I'll do and give
And help the world to better live,
And all my friends I will forgive
    If I have time.

I'll love my children, friends and wife
I'll help to rid the world of strife,
I'll live a greater, fuller life
    If I have time.

I'll travel north, south, east or west
And read the books that I love best,
I'll seek the things the loveliest
    If I have time.

With the children I'll romp and play
Thru woods and fields we'll stroll some day,
We'll get acquainted on the way
    If I have time.

The kite I'll fix, the doll I'll mend
The child on me can sure depend,
As thru this life, his way he'll wend
    If I have time.

I'll listen to the bird's song and cry
I'll see the sunset in the sky,
The moon and stars gleaming on high
    If I have time.

Of life's treasures — I've wanted more
Soon life's journey here will be o'er,
I'll leave it for the other shore
    If I have time.

MOVING

When one has the desire and urge
    Conditions we must improve
All it seems there is to do is
    To find a place to move.

So then we wash and fold and wrap
    In basket, box and tub
Those fragile dainties which we love
    Our household we turn — hub bub.

So we just handle everything
    Carefully as we can
And then just back up to the door
    To crowd things into the van.

"Good-byes", are so cheerlessly said
    To the new home we go
Just wondering with awe
    How those people stood conditions so.

There is that short window
    We must make it into a door
Take the kitchen so old and worn
    It must have a new floor.

About six inches left or right
    To move that old partition
For these old rooms must be
    Just right and in good condition.

Just to rake and dig and replant
    Through the yard to the gate
Then to scrub, scrape and paint
    You newly decorate.

All the friends, the old and the new
　　Some you thought had forgotten you
But they'll all come calling now,
　　When your home — it is new.

Now all you do is settle down
　　Living year after year
With but a very few changes
　　That does seem to appear.

Until of these same conditions
　　One comes to disapprove
Just go and find another place
　　So you can up and move.

A LITTLE CHURCH ON THE CORNER STANDS

Towering heavenward so high
    As a silhouette in the sky
So stately and tall, the steeple
    Beckoning to all the people
Ever ready for their demands
    A little church on the corner stands.

Softly and sweet the bell does toll
    A welcome for many a soul
Longing for some kind word or song
    As thru this world one moves along
For something finer one does search
    On the corner, in that little church.

It matters not the race or creed
    All must forsake the personal greed
War, strife and anger brought to cease
    May love and fellowship bring peace
Be it thru a hymn or a prayer
    In a little church standing there.

Across the hills, plains or valley
    In a mansion, hut or alley
May grace and glory still one find
    And be a help to all mankind
And that forever throughout our lands
    A little church on the corner stands.

OUR DEAR OLD U.S.A.

Our many people love liberty and peace
    Also are wishing that
        this cruel war would cease
But just let someone
    make a ruthless attack
The enemies will all know
    how we react.
A pretty price they'll have to pay
    Our dear old U S A.

Ours is not vast riches
    not broad lands to gain
We want freedom and liberty
    to remain
It is not crowned rulers
    nor dictators few
We want our democracy
    so tried and true
Our country we will not betray
We love our dear old U S A.

Some countries may depend upon
    man made might
But let our nation adhere
    to Divine Right
Years ago, for us this
    liberty was bought
By and with that precious blood
    of those who fought
We'll keep behind them night and day
    For our dear old U S A.

Many times we have found
    it in danger lies
That within our bounds
    there lurk dangerous spies
This means to us
    much sorrow and worry
But we are all united
    for Old Glory
Sacrifices we will obey
    For our dear old U S A.

No blessed souls would
    we want to enslave
There is nothing to gain
    but so much to save
To save our country, all means
    we will employ
And keep these precious privileges
    we now enjoy
Our Stars and Stripes are here to stay
    In our dear old U S A.

So this glorious heritage which is ours
We will keep it free
    from over ruling powers
And false propaganda
    let us never fear
But for the red, the white and blue
    let us cheer
Just count our blessings day by day
    In our dear old U S A.

EDNA IRENE HOLLAND

At eighteen.